Vor Gott sind alle Menschen gleich

1 **Pierre Mendell**
Vor Gott sind alle Menschen gleich
1995 DE

VORWORT

Entwicklungspolitische und ökologische Fragestellungen sind aufgrund ihrer globalen Dimension und ethischen Brisanz heute ein viel diskutiertes Medienthema. Unter dem Schlagwort *Corporate Social Responsibility* bemühen sich auch Wirtschaftsunternehmen zunehmend um soziales und umweltpolitisches Engagement. Umso mehr gestaltet es sich als besondere Herausforderung, im kommerziellen Werbeumfeld den Blick der Passanten für soziale Anliegen mittels des Plakats zu fesseln. Neben den traditionellen Auftraggebern sozialer Plakate – Hilfswerke, Menschenrechts- und Umweltschutzorganisationen – zeichnen engagierte Gestalter und vereinzelt kommerzielle Unternehmen als Absender. So verschieden ihre Ziele, so unterschiedlich sind Bildrhetorik und Argumentationsstrategien der hier versammelten internationalen Plakate mit Schweizer Schwerpunkt seit 1980.

Im Plakat entwicklungspolitischer Organisationen hat der Hungerbauch zwar abgedankt. Der vorübergehend versuchten Strategie, hilfsbedürftige Menschen als sich emanzipiert für ein humanes Leben einsetzende Individuen zu zeigen, blieb der Spendenerfolg jedoch weitgehend versagt. Not muss sich offensichtlich doch visuell manifestieren – sei es auch in sublimierter Form. Die Rollenverteilung von edlem Spender und dankbarem Empfänger, die die Frage nach Mitverantwortung bewusst ausklammert, bewährt sich noch immer am besten für den Griff zum Portemonnaie. Der Pragmatismus sozialer Institutionen beweist sich heute aber auch nicht selten in der Übernahme der massenmedial wirksamen PR-Ästhetik der Konsumwerbung – ohne dabei vor Geschmacklosigkeit zurückzuschrecken. Der Fokus des im Eigenauftrag gestalteten Plakats engagierter Grafikdesigner liegt auf Aufklärung. Dabei offenbart sich beispielhaft die Schwierigkeit, komplexe sozio-politische, ökonomische und ökologische Bezüge in mediumsgerechter, knapper Form zu transportieren. Neben gelungenen, innovativen Metaphern häufen sich auch hier bildliche Klischees. Verschlüsselte Botschaften, die Emotionalität und Rationalität auf hohem formalem Niveau verbinden, finden hingegen oft nur ein eingeweihtes Publikum. Im kommerziellen Plakat ist Oliviero Toscanis umstrittene «Schockwerbung» für Benetton bis heute ohne Nachfolge geblieben. In Gegenüberstellung mit Michael von Graffenrieds jüngst präsentiertem Plakatzyklus aus Kamerun wird hier exemplarisch der Frage nachgegangen, was der andere Blick auf fremde Kulturen und Menschen und die unterschiedliche Auftraggeberschaft beim Publikum bewirken.

Die Kommunikation sozialer Botschaften im Plakat erweist sich oftmals als Gratwanderung zwischen Verharmlosung, Banalisierung, Ästhetisierung und Schock oder intellektueller Unlesbarkeit. Darin spiegelt sich allerdings auch das Rezeptionsverhalten der Betrachtenden. So verstanden, sind die gezeigten Plakate nicht zuletzt auch eine Aufforderung, eigene Seh- und Denkgewohnheiten zu reflektieren und sich auf neue Bilder einzulassen.

Bettina Richter

COLLECTION

HELP!

20

SOZIALE APPELLE
APPEALS TO SOCIAL CONSCIENCE

Herausgegeben von / Edited by Bettina Richter

Essay von / by Sønke Gau und / and Katharina Schlieben

MUSEUM FÜR GESTALTUNG ZÜRICH
PLAKATSAMMLUNG / POSTER COLLECTION

LARS MÜLLER PUBLISHERS

FOREWORD

Given their global dimensions and ethical urgency, development and ecology are frequent topics of discussion in the contemporary media. Under the motto "corporate social responsibility," private enterprises also attempt to certify their social and environmental commitment. Inevitably, one of the special challenges facing us vis-à-vis our commercialized environment is to use posters to catch the eyes of passers-by, thereby calling attention to social issues. Found today alongside the traditional commissioners of socially-oriented posters (i.e. relief, human rights, and environmental organizations) are politically engaged designers and exceptional commercial enterprises. Reflecting the different respective goals of these constituencies are the contrasting visual rhetorics and argumentative strategies of the international posters gathered together in this publication, with its focus on Switzerland since 1980.

The formerly ubiquitous bloated belly has vanished from the posters of development organizations. At the same time, the strategy – pursued only briefly – of displaying the needy as emancipated individuals who agitate for a more humane life has encountered little success in soliciting contributions. Evidently, the plight of the needy must be manifested visually – if only in sublimated form. The division of roles between noble benefactor and grateful beneficiary, one that deliberately excluded questions of shared responsibility, remains the tried and tested one when it comes to gaining access to people's wallets. In many cases, the pragmatism of relief organizations is manifested in the adoption of the same consumerist aesthetic that has proven so effective in the mass media – and without shying away from questionable taste. Consciousness-raising is the main focus of posters produced by committed graphic designers on their own initiative. Such work testifies in an exemplary way to the difficulties involved in conveying complex sociopolitical, economic, and ecological concerns in an abbreviated form while doing justice to the medium. Accumulating alongside successful, innovative metaphors are visual clichés. Encoded messages which connect emotion and rationality on an elevated formal plane, on the other hand, often reach only an initiated public, i.e. previously sensitized individuals. In the field of the commercial poster, Oliviero Toscani's controversial "shock ads" for Benetton remain without successors to date. Posed in an exemplary fashion via a juxtaposition of his work with Michael von Graffenried's recent poster cycle from Cameroon is the following question: What can various clients achieve by directing the public's gaze toward foreign cultures and peoples?

The communication of social messages via the poster is often revealed as a tightrope walk between the innocuous, the banal, the aestheticized, the shocking, and the unintelligible. Also implicated in the communication process is viewer/receiver behavior, and thus the posters on display represent above all a challenge to reflect on our own visual and mental habits, to open ourselves to new realities.

Bettina Richter

UNITED COLORS
OF BENETTON.

2 **Oliviero Toscani**
United Colors of Benetton. / Benetton Group S.p.A.
1992 IT

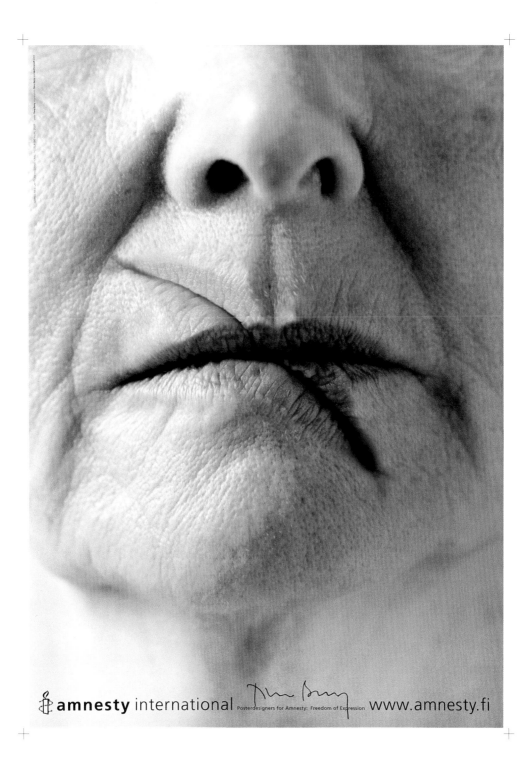

3 **Timo Berry**
Posterdesigners for Amnesty:
Freedom of Expression / Amnesty International
2003 FI

4 **Grapus**
Rich − Poor / Artis
1989 FR

Is your baby safe?

Save your child from the polluted water.

5 **Naoki Hirai**
Is your baby safe?
2001 JP

6 **Lex Drewinski**
Racism / Friedensinitiative Berlin
1993 DE

7 **Mitsuo Katsui**
AIR – I'm here / Japan Graphic Designers Association
1993 JP

WER APPELLIERT WARUM UND WIE AN WEN?

Eine Frage der Übersetzungsstrategien in Hinblick auf die Ökonomie der Aufmerksamkeit

Sønke Gau und Katharina Schlieben

«Wissensgesellschaft» und «Informationszeitalter» sind viel verwendete Schlagwörter gegenwärtiger Zeitdiagnosen. Sie verweisen auf einen tief greifenden Wandel der Wirtschafts- und Gesellschaftsstrukturen. Informationen sind durch technische Entwicklungen – zumindest in den sogenannten «westlichen» Gesellschaften – wesentlich einfacher zugänglich. Jedes neue Medium (Bücher, Zeitungen, Radio, Fernsehen, Internet etc.) potenziert die zur Verfügung stehenden Informationen. War es in früheren Zeiten schwierig, an Informationen zu gelangen, so geht es mittlerweile eher um Mechanismen, die multimediale Informationsflut zu kanalisieren bzw. aus ihr auszuwählen. Informationen sind zwar eine Grundvoraussetzung für Wissen, aber eben nur in einer sinnvollen Verknüpfung: In ihrer ausgewählten und aufbereiteten Form kann aus der Verbindung von Informationen Wissen entstehen. Um diesen Auswahl- und Verknüpfungsprozess leisten zu können, bedarf es einer gewissen «Aufmerksamkeit». Aufmerksamkeit, so hat es Georg Franck in seinem Buch *Ökonomie der Aufmerksamkeit*[1] beschrieben, ist in der Informations- und Wissensgesellschaft zu einer knappen Ressource geworden. Da auf allen Ebenen um Aufmerksamkeit geworben wird, sie aber nicht proportional steigerbar ist, gewinnt sie nach den Marktgesetzen von Angebot und Nachfrage an Wert. Der Wert von Aufmerksamkeit unter ökonomischen Gesichtspunkten beschränkt sich dabei jedoch nicht nur auf die Werbewirtschaft, sondern ist von Bedeutung für alle gesellschaftlichen Belange, die auf Öffentlichkeiten angewiesen sind, um auf ihre Anliegen hinzuweisen. Sie alle stehen somit in unmittelbarer Konkurrenz um die knappe Ressource Aufmerksamkeit. Die Frage, mit welchen Medien und welchen Strategien sich Inhalte, Anliegen und Handlungsaufforderungen am besten kommunizieren lassen, ist somit auch eine Frage nach der Form der Vermittlung. Es bedarf einer Entscheidung, welches Medium oder welche Medien man für die Vermittlung der Botschaft nutzen möchte und welche Strategie man innerhalb des Mediums nutzt, um Aufmerksamkeit zu erzielen. Da aber sowohl die Anzahl der Medien als auch die der bekannten Strategien beschränkt ist, kommt es zwischen den Vermittlungsformen unterschiedlicher gesellschaftlicher Bereiche (Politik, Kultur, Werbung etc.) zwangsläufig zu Parallelen und Überschneidungen, aber auch zu Abgrenzungen, Adaptionen und Verfremdungen.

Beobachten lassen sich diese gegenseitigen Bezugsnahmen in jedem Medium, besonders deutlich werden sie aber im Plakat, da es in seinen Möglichkeiten der Informationsvermittlung auf einfache Lesbarkeit angewiesen ist. Die grosse «Reichweite» von Plakaten im sogenannten öffentlichen Raum resultiert aus dem Umstand, dass man je nach Platzierung der Plakate quasi zwangsläufig an ihnen vorbeikommt – da das Vorbeikommen aber nicht per se auch eine gesteigerte Aufmerksamkeit zur

Folge hat, bedarf es einer auffälligen, einprägsamen Gestaltung von Text- und Bild-
information, unabhängig davon, ob man nun eine Ware verkaufen, für eine politische
Partei werben oder einen sozialen Appell vermitteln möchte. Gestaltung ist in diesem
Zusammenhang weniger als ästhetische Kategorie interessant, sondern vielmehr als
Repräsentationssystem mit inhärenten Beziehungen zwischen Visualität, Medialität,
Identität, Ökonomie und Macht, das Fragen nach kulturellen, sozialen, ökonomischen
und politischen Motivationen und Strategien aufwirft.

Spätestens seit den 1980er Jahren mit dem Einzug der Grünen in die europäischen
Regierungsparlamente, einem Wissen um Waldsterben und Tschernobyl, einer zweiten
Massentourismuswelle, einer unaufhaltsamen Globalisierung, die ihre Auswirkungen
und marktökonomischen Gewinne zu rechtfertigen versucht, den übernationalstaatli-
chen Entwicklungshilfeprogrammen, den ersten Klimakonferenzen und einer Arbeits-
losigkeit, die nicht mit der Frage um Arbeitsmigration in Zusammenhang gebracht
wurde, sind Fragestellungen, Ängste, Handlungsbedarf im unternehmerischen, politischen und individuellen Denken präsent. Auf der Suche nach sozialen und politischen
Appellen sind diese zum Teil plakativen, hilflosen, solidarisierenden Aufrufe in die Kin-
derzimmer einer ganzen Generation eingezogen und haben sich im Bewusstsein des
alltäglichen Lebens verankert: «Rettet den Baum», «Frieden schaffen ohne Waffen»,
«Atomkraft? Nein Danke» – so und ähnlich stand es auf den Plakaten und Aufklebern,
die wie Trophäen des Wissens über soziale Ungerechtigkeit und notwendigen Umden-
kens über dem Bett hingen.

Die Slogans sollten motivieren, einer unterschwelligen Zukunftsangst mit Handlung
zu begegnen, Solidarität schaffen oder ein schlechtes Gewissen verursachen. Die
Appellfunktion und -rhetorik wurde und wird hierbei von staatlicher Seite genauso
wie von nicht-staatlichen Initiativen produziert und genutzt. Auffällig ist, dass nur
wenige eine subversivere, differenziertere Text- und Bildsprache nutzen, vielmehr
ging und geht es darum, ein kollektives Bewusstsein zu erreichen. Die Frage war nur,
wer spricht warum und wie zu wem?

Seit den 80ern spiegeln die sozialen Appelle im Plakat eine Geschichte wider, die
über politische Diskussionen und über die mitwirkenden und verantwortlichen Akteu-
rInnen und ihre jeweiligen Sprachen einiges zu erzählen hat. Aber nicht nur das, im
Besonderen interessiert auch die Frage, wie werden wir angesprochen, auf welche
Weise werden Sprecher- und Empfängerperspektiven konstruiert, verschoben, ent-
larvt oder ausgetauscht. Ein einseitiges Kommunikationsmodell (Sender/Empfänger)
wird hier zugunsten der vorweggehenden Frage nach Identität- und Differenzerfahrungen der Rezipienten/Produzenten gestört.

Die post-colonial studies (im Dialog mit gender und psychoanalytischen Studien)
haben hybride Identitätskonstruktionen und Fragen nach Übersetzung in Bezug auf

Differenzerfahrungen zum jeweils «Anderen» untersucht. Wobei Differenzerfahrung nicht mehr in einem «Aussen» oder einem «Anderen» gesucht, sondern im «Eigenen» neu bestimmt wird. Julia Kristeva etwa formulierte diese Differenzerfahrung in *Fremde sind wir uns selbst*[2] als eine intersubjektive Konstruktion, welche das «Andere» als mein eigenes Unbewusstsein definiert. Eine Reihe von Plakatinitiativen dekonstruieren den angenommenen identitären Mythos und verweisen auf das uns «Fremde im Eigenen».

So verkündet zum Beispiel die Selbstanklage in Gestaltung einer Todesanzeige einer Greenpeace-Kampagne von 1994 Folgendes: «Ich ruiniere das Klima, weil meine Kraftwerke jährlich 100 Millionen Tonnen CO_2 in die Luft schleudern», abgebildet ist Dr. Dietmar Kuhnt, Vorstandsvorsitzender der RWE Energie AG. Greenpeace übernimmt hier stellvertretend den subjektivierten Appell an das eigene Gewissen oder Unbewusstsein, das Ungesagte, Verschwiegene wird öffentlich gemacht. In einer Plakatkampagne der Initiative Anschläge.de im Rahmen der Reihe «Hier spricht Barmbek – Barmbek.tv» fragt die Rentnerin Paula stellvertretend für viele Leidensgenossinnen einer schweigenden Mehrheit: «Mal ganz ehrlich, können Sie mit 100 € im Monat auskommen?» 72 Sie fordert ein Eingeständnis, das Altersarmut als ein Problem vieler NachbarInnen artikuliert und nicht als ein peinliches Schweigen einzelner Betroffener. Das Autorenplakat von Roland Piltz und Aisha Ronniger folgt einer anderen Strategie: Durch die Montage verschiedener (auch gender-konnotierter) Porträtabschnitte und Textfragmente «New York – Vladimir – Arbeitslos» in einem Siebdruckverfahren wird einer oberflächlich identitären Vorstellung einer Subjektkonstruktion widersprochen 83. Ausschnitte bieten Identifikationsmöglichkeiten an, andere nicht, was dazu führt, dass Identifikationsphantasmen befragt werden müssen.

Koloniale Praxen schreiben sich fort, so beschreibt es unter anderem Kien Nghi Ha in seiner Publikation *Ethnizität und Migration*[3]. Trotz formeller politischer Unabhängigkeit von westlichen Kolonialmächten setzen sich koloniales Blickregime und Machtkonstellationen fort, strukturieren gesellschaftliche Verhältnisse und reproduzieren sich in ihnen. Dies gilt auch für manche Plakatkampagne: Besonders deutlich wird es, wenn es um die Frage einer globalen Mobilität geht: die einen migrieren, die anderen reisen. Klaus Staeck reagiert in einem von ihm gestalteten Plakat auf diese bipolare Wahrnehmung mit folgendem Slogan: «In jedem Urlaub werden Millionen Deutsche zu Ausländern» 114. Ein «weisses» Pärchen einsam vor einer Südseekulisse. Ihre Schablonenhaftigkeit verstärkt den Text insofern, dass sie wie in das Szenario hinein collagiert erscheinen, nicht mit dem Kontext, sondern nur miteinander verbunden. Dieses Fehlen von Austausch oder Aufeinander-Zugehen thematisiert aus einer anderen Perspektive Segregationsprozesse in deutschen Städten oder urbanen Randgebieten, wie etwa das Plakat von Gunter Rambow: «Deutschland den Deutschen – Frankfurt den Frankfurtern – Seckbach den Seckbachern – Herr

Meier dem Herrn Meier – Rassismus macht einsam». 76 So heisst es in fünf roten Textbalken, die ein Porträt einer Person vermutlich migrantischen Hintergrundes gitterhaft verdecken. Von «Deutschland, Frankfurt, Seckbach» bis zu «Herr Meier» wird hier eine Lesekette vermittelt, die letztlich stellvertretend für viele «Meiers» beim Individuum Herr Meier endet, der sich durch ausgrenzende und sich abgrenzende gesellschaftliche Haltungen selbst einsam macht und sich damit selbst stellvertretend hinter den Gittern erblicken könnte. Die aus Angst produzierte Einsamkeit, sei es die der TouristInnen, der MigrantInnen oder der NationalistInnen, sind wiederkehrende Topoi in Plakatentwürfen, die sich mit Identität und Ethnizität auseinandersetzen.

Das Umdrehen der Sprecherperspektive ist eine weitere Strategie, Einflüsse einer kolonialen geschichtlichen Matrix bewusst zu machen und eine Selbstreflexion über subjektive Wissensstandpunkte zu provozieren: Das Plakat von Meta-Cultura, Zürich 94, beispielsweise zeigt eine Wandmalerei der Hima aus Uganda, kombiniert mit der Aussage eines Dorfchefs aus Mali: «Die Weissen denken zuviel» (bezugnehmend auf den Titel des legendären Buchs von Paul Parin, Fritz Morgenthaler und Goldy Parin-Matthèy).[4] Das Plakat, initiiert von Helvetas, Schweizer Gesellschaft für Entwicklung und Zusammenarbeit, irritiert in mehrfacher Hinsicht: Unter der Aussage des Dorfchefs steht: «Ureinwohner haben uns viel zu sagen. Im Helvetas Spezialheft *Ureinwohner* kommen sie zu Wort». Durch die Verwendung des Begriffs «Ureinwohner» wird bewusst oder unbewusst der Wissenskontext des «Dorfchefs» romantisiert, archaisiert und gleichzeitig exotisiert. Der zunächst interessante Perspektivenwechsel läuft Gefahr, unglaubhaft und pädagogisch zu werden. Ähnlich ergeht es einem in der Plakatkampagne der Swissaid: «Spielen Sie Wilhelm Tell» 120. Die Bildadaption des heroischen Wilhelm-Tell-Gestus, der an die eigene mythische Befreiung und Identität erinnern soll, schlägt vor, sich mit dem Abschuss einer Mango oder Ananas mithilfe von Pfeil und Bogen selbst zu befreien. Untertitelt ist das Bildszenario mit «Spenden Sie Freiheit. Hilfe, die weiterhilft.» Hilfe zur Selbsthilfe, die dank Friedrich Schillers Drama 1804 zu einem «helvetischen Verfahren» wurde: Aber entpuppt sich die Idee der Hilfe zur Selbsthilfe hier nicht rhetorisch als ein «Macht es so wie wir?» Oder führt die Kampagne nicht gar zu einer Handlungsunfähigkeit – selbst wenn davon auszugehen ist, dass die Tellkampagne zur Selbsthilfe ironisch gemeint ist und sich selbstreflexiv befragt?

Anders agiert die Stiftung gegen Rassismus und Antisemitismus. «Woher haben die Kosovo-Albaner ihre Autoradios?» – «Aus dem Fachgeschäft, wie die meisten Schweizer auch» 116. Oder «Was machen Thailänderinnen, wenn es dunkel wird?» – «Licht wie die meisten Schweizer auch» 118. Ihr Fragen- und Antwortspiel ist so plakativ gestellt und die bildhaften Fratzen so comic-haft oder märchenbuchähnlich, dass man nicht umhin kann zu schmunzeln. Gleichzeitig erinnern sie an eine Witztradition, die mit «Was machen die Chinesen, wenn…?» begann. Die Text- und Bildebene greift hier auf bekannte Codes zurück, die subversiv modifiziert werden. Roland Barthes hat einmal gefragt: «Ist die beste Subversion nicht die, Codes zu entstellen statt sie zu zerstören?»[5] Dieser Idee konnten sich viele künstlerische Gruppierungen anschliessen, wie etwa die Aktionen und medialen Interventionen der Kommunikationsguerilla oder die Spassguerilla, die versucht haben, medialen Bild- und Textsprachen subversiv eine andere Bedeutung zu geben.

Interessanterweise bedienen sich nur wenige Initiativen subversiver Strategien. Vielmehr wird zu einer Art Selbstdisziplinierung aufgerufen, in einer gouvernementalen Redeweise, die an das Subjekt appelliert und politische Rationalität fordert. So zum Beispiel Woody Pirtle, der in seiner Plakatserie an das kollektive Bewusstsein appelliert und die Menschenrechte in Erinnerung ruft: «From the Universal Declaration of Human Rights», hier zum Beispiel «Article 25 – Everyone Has the Right to an Adequate Standard of Living» 22. Manche möchten hingegen eher eine rein ökonomische Logik verdeutlichen, wie etwa das Plakat der Ogilvy & Mather AG, Zürich: Die Abbildung eines gefüllten Bierglases ist mit folgendem Text überschrieben: «Damit versorgen Sie ein Kind in Haiti einen Monat lang mit einer warmen Mahlzeit. – Caritas – Not hat viele Gesichter. Spendenkonto 60-700-4» 119.

Das Mass an Konventionalität und Seriosität der Text- und Bildaussagen steigt im Fall von sozialen Anliegen proportional zur «Ernsthaftigkeit» des jeweiligen Themas – im Gegensatz zu gängiger kommerzieller Werbung, die uns durch Prestigeteilhabe am Image des zu erwerbenden Produkts ein glückliches Leben, Reichtum, Schönheit etc. suggeriert und sich oft noch nicht einmal um Realitätsnähe bemüht. Dieser Mechanismus spiegelt die unausgesprochene Unterscheidung zwischen kommerzieller Kommunikation/Werbung und kulturellem oder politischem Diskurs. Es wird eine Medienkompetenz vorausgesetzt, aufgrund derer angenommen wird, dass in der Regel niemand die Versprechen und Aussagen der Werbung mit der Realität verwechselt, während sich politische Aussagen und Appelle von NGOs und anderen Initiativen meist explizit um einen Realitätsbezug bemühen. Wie ausgeprägt diese Grenzziehung ist, lässt sich am besten nachvollziehen, wenn man jene Fälle betrachtet, bei denen diese Übereinkunft gebrochen wurde.

Das wohl mit Abstand prominenteste Beispiel in diesem Kontext ist die von dem Fotografen Oliviero Toscani entwickelte Werbekampagne für die Modefirma Benetton, die weltweit für Aufsehen sorgte s. S. 64ff. Während das Unternehmen darauf beharrte, mit seiner Werbung gesellschaftliche Verantwortung wahrnehmen zu wollen, indem es im Rahmen seiner Kampagne nicht seine Produkte bewerbe, sondern auf politische Themen, Tabus und gesellschaftliche Missstände hinweise, beanstandeten die KritikerInnen, dass es unethisch sei, das Leid anderer Menschen zur Umsatzsteigerung eines Unternehmens zu nutzen. Die Kontroverse veranschaulichte, dass die Benetton-Kampagne mit ihrer plakativen Zurschaustellung von

Bildern über Krieg 101, HIV/Aids 100, Tod, Rassismus 97, Umweltverschmutzung 57, Todesstrafe 73, 75, Flüchtlingselend 2 etc. offensichtlich bestimmte unausgesprochene Grenzziehungen verletzte. Dieselben Bilder, die in Nachrichtensendungen zum täglichen Geschäft gehören – etwa eine ölüberzogene Ente im Ölteppich schwimmend 57 –, sollen im Zusammenhang mit einer Werbekampagne nicht gezeigt werden.

Dass die Bewertung dieser Kampagne höchst komplex ist, zeigt der Umstand, dass sie einerseits Proteste und Gerichtsverfahren auslöste und andererseits in einigen Ländern zur Aidsaufklärung und für Anti-Rassismuskampagnen genutzt – und selbstverständlich in vielen musealen Plakatsammlungen archiviert und ausgestellt wurde. Eins ist aber sicher: Im Sinne einer Ökonomie der Aufmerksamkeit hat sich die Kampagne auf jeden Fall gerechnet. Aus einer italienischen Strickwarenfirma wurde eine der bekanntesten Marken der Welt.

Die eingangs formulierte Frage «Wer appelliert warum und wie an wen?» ist im Hinblick auf soziale Appelle im Plakat notwendig, um zu erfahren, durch welche Motivationen und Strategien spezifische Bild- und Textsprachen in den Vordergrund gestellt und von wem sie an wen adressiert werden. Strategien, welche die Sprecherperspektive thematisieren, oder subversive und überaffirmative Verdeutlichungen ermöglichen einen Blick hinter die plakativen Oberflächen und lassen auf einen zweiten Blick Rückschlüsse auf die Motivation und Anliegen der Plakatgestalterinnen und Plakatgestalter bzw. deren Auftraggeber zu.

1 Georg Franck, *Ökonomie der Aufmerksamkeit. Ein Entwurf*, München/Wien 1998.
2 Julia Kristeva, *Fremde sind wir uns selbst*, deutsche Erstausgabe, Frankfurt am Main 1990.
3 Kien Nghi Ha, *Ethnizität und Migration*, Münster 1999.
4 Paul Parin, Fritz Morgenthaler, Goldy Parin-Matthèy, *Die Weissen denken zuviel*, Zürich 1963.
5 Roland Barthes, *Sade – Fourier – Loyola*, deutsche Ausgabe, Frankfurt am Main 1986.

think globally · act locally

1990 · Earth Day

迷彩色の地球はごめんだぜ!!

いま地球上には広島に投下された原爆の約150万倍の破壊力
をもつ量の核兵器が貯蔵されている。陸にも、海にも、空にも…
いかなる核大国も地球をめちゃめちゃにする権利はないはずだ。

NO ONE WANTS A CAMOUFLAGED EARTH !!
There are nuclear bombs which have one and a half million
times the destructive power of the nuclear bomb which was
dropped on Hiroshima stored on the earth today. No great
nuclear power has any right to completely devastate the
earth, either on land, on sea, or in the sky.

1986   INTERNATIONAL YEAR OF PEACE

THERE IS ONLY ONE EARTH... SAVE IT

C. P. R. ENVIRONMENTAL EDUCATION CENTRE
THE C. P. RAMASAMI AIYAR FOUNDATION
1A, ELDAMS ROAD, MADRAS 600 018
PRINTED ON TREE-FREE PAPER

8 **Norman Clayton**
think globally – act locally – 1990 – Earth Day /
Environmental Protection Agency, 1990 US

9 **Lanny Sommese**
1986 / International Year of Peace
1986 US

10 **Hirokatsu Hijikata**
No one wants a camouflaged earth!!
ca. 1990 JP

11 **Anonym**
There is only one earth...Save it / Environmental
Education Centre Madras, ca. 1996 IN

12 **Klaus Staeck**
Die Mietsache ist schonend zu behandeln
und in gutem Zustand zurückzugeben
1983 DE

13 **Gérard Paris-Clavel**
Money World
1992 FR

Eigentlich sieht die Welt so aus.

Die Karte zeigt den Lebensmittelkonsum der Länder Europas und Afrikas: Über 920 Millionen Menschen hungern. Helfen Sie uns die Verhältnisse zu verändern, denn das Recht auf Nahrung braucht ein gutes Klima. PC 60-707 707-2

BROT FÜR ALLE
FASTENOPFER
In Zusammenarbeit mit Partner sein

www.rechtaufnahrung.ch

14 **Spillmann, Felser, Leo Burnett AG**
Eigentlich sieht die Welt so aus.
Brot für Alle / Fastenopfer
2009 CH

CARITAS

Hngr.

Alle 5 Sekunden reisst der Hunger ein Kind aus dem Leben.

www.caritas.ch
Spendenkonto 60-7000-4

15 **Spinas Gemperle GmbH**
Hngr. Alle 5 Sekunden reisst der Hunger
ein Kind aus dem Leben. / Caritas
2008 CH

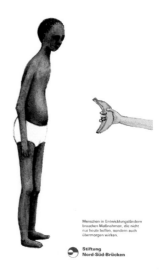

16 **Hoffmann, York & Compton**
There are worse things in life than going to bed
hungry. / Hunger Task Force, 1991 US

17 **Peter Cohen**
"Finish your food" / Coalition for the Homeless
1990 US

18 **Ina Hattenhauer**
Menschen in Entwicklungsländern brauchen Massnahmen. / Stiftung Nord-Süd-Brücken, 2005 DE

19 **Publicis Werbeagentur AG**
Wenn Kinder sich nicht wehren können.
Help / Terre des hommes, 2006 CH

THE BREAD IS FOR *PEACE*

戦争に使うパンはない

sh are

20 **Masuteru Aoba**
The bread is for *peace*
1984 JP

21 **Pierre Mendell Design Studio**
share
2004 DE

22 **Pentagram Design New York**
From the Universal Declaration of Human Rights –
Article 25 – Everyone Has the Right to an Adequate
Standard of Living / Amnesty International
2002 US

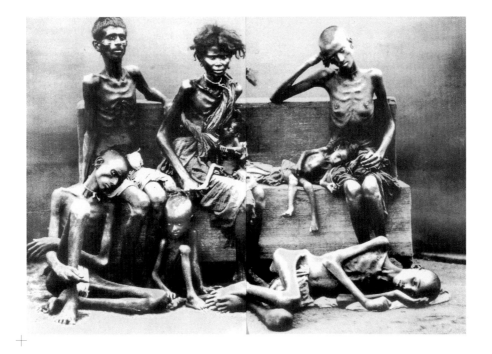

23 **Teemu Mäki**
Artikla 29 – Ihmisoikeuksien Yleismaailmallinen Julistus
60 Vuotta / Amnesty International
2008 FI

24 **Cyan**
1994 DE

25 **Klaus Staeck**
Das Neue Pal / Schlachtfrisch aus der Dose.
1977 DE

SUDAN

26 **Luba Lukova**
War Crime / International Anti-Poverty Law Center
1999 US

27 **Tiitu Takalo**
Artikla 25 – Ihmisoikeuksien Yleismaailmallinen Julistus
60 Vuotta / Amnesty International, 2008 FI

28 **Luba Lukova**
Hunger Crime / International Anti-Poverty Law Center
1999 US

29 **Luba Lukova**
Sudan / International Anti-Poverty Law Center
1999 US

Save the Children Organization.

30 **U. G. Sato**
Save hungry children / Save the Children Organization
1998 JP

Schnelle medizinische Hilfe. www.msf.ch MÉDECINS SANS FRONTIÈRES

the muslim government in
the north was clashing
with the christian rebels
from the south. now the
rebels are killing eachother.
those caught in the middle
die a little slower.

Smoking in public receives a more violent reaction nowadays than stories like this. Where has our perspective gone? NON SMOKERS FOR THE RIGHTS OF SMOKERS

It was a typical mother
and son outing to the
movies. Except twenty
minutes into the film
the boy splatters his
mum's brains over the
seats with a revolver.

31 **Publicis Werbeagentur AG**
Schnelle medizinische Hilfe./Médecins sans Frontières
2006 CH

32 **Anonym**
Non-Smokers for the Rights of Smokers/
Humanist Association of Hongkong, 1996 HK

33 **Anonym**
Non-Smokers for the Rights of Smokers/
Humanist Association of Hongkong, 1996 HK

34 **Gaudenz Tscharner AG**
L'acqua fonte di vita – Helvetas aiuta i paesi del Terzo
Mondo. E voi? / Helvetas, 1986 CH

35 **Anonym**
We teach / Internationales Komitee vom Roten Kreuz
ca. 2005 CH

36 **Spinas Gemperle GmbH**
Für 1,1 Milliarden Menschen kein Witz. / Helvetas
2008 CH

37 **Anonym**
We quench thirst / Internationales Komitee vom
Roten Kreuz, ca. 2005 CH

38 **Scherer Kleiber Creative Direction AG**
Mutter spielen, weil man keine hat. / United Nations
International Children's Emergency Fund, 1988 CH

39 **Publicis Werbeagentur AG**
Was wir unter Kinderarbeit verstehen. /
Migros-Genossenschafts-Bund, 2006 CH

40 **Homberger & Minet, Graphic Design**
«Ich fragte, weshalb ich nicht zur Schule dürfte.
Es hiess, ich solle arbeiten. Ich arbeite immer bis spät
in die Nacht.» / Terre des hommes
2004 CH

Es gibt einen Weg aus jedem Unrecht.

Terre des hommes
Kinderhilfe · www.tdh.ch

Wir kämpfen gegen Kinderarbeit.

Dank Ihnen leben Jugendliche in Brasilien vom Mais.

Statt vom Müll.

Spendenkonto 40-260-2   terre des hommes schweiz   www.terredeshommes.ch

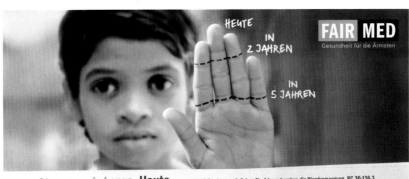

HEUTE
IN 2 JAHREN
IN 5 JAHREN

FAIR MED
Gesundheit für die Ärmsten

Stoppen wir Lepra. Heute.   Mit 40 Franken ermöglichen Sie 4 Leprakranken die Wundversorgung. PC 30-136-3

41 **Publicis Werbeagentur AG**
Es gibt einen Weg aus jedem Unrecht. Wir kämpfen
gegen Kinderarbeit. / Terre des hommes, 2007 CH

43 **Spinas Gemperle GmbH**
Stoppen wir Lepra. / Fairmed
2009 CH

42 **Spinas Gemperle GmbH**
Dank Ihnen leben Jugendliche in Brasilien vom Mais.
Statt vom Müll. / Terre des hommes, 2007 CH

WHO APPEALS TO WHOM, AND HOW, AND TO WHAT ENDS?
On Strategies of Translation Vis-à-Vis the Economy of Attention

Sønke Gau and Katharina Schlieben

The slogans "knowledge society" and "information age"—used frequently in diagnoses of contemporary life—point toward far-reaching transformations in economic and social structures. At least in so-called Western societies, technological developments have rendered information vastly more accessible. Each new medium (the book, the newspaper, radio, television, the Internet, etc.) has exponentially increased the quantity of available information. If in earlier times information was difficult to obtain, by now it is a question of designing mechanisms to channel or select from the multimedia flood. To be sure, information is a fundamental precondition for knowledge, but only provided there are expedient linkages: once it has been pre-selected and processed, knowledge can emerge from the interlinking of units of information. Required for the achievement of such selection processes and linkages is a certain "attentiveness." As described by Georg Franck in his book *Ökonomie der Aufmerksamkeit* (Economy of attentiveness),[1] attentiveness has come to be a resource in short supply. Despite the fact that our attention is solicited on all levels, it cannot be increased proportionally; consequently, its value increases according to market laws of supply and demand. From an economic standpoint, the value of attentiveness is not restricted to the advertising industry, but is instead significant for social campaigns that rely on the public sphere to call attention to their concerns. All of these are in direct competition for the same scarce resource. Questions concerning which medium and which strategies are best suited to conveying specific contents, concerns, and calls to action are also, consequently, questions about forms of intervention. It is necessary to decide which medium/media can best convey a given message, and which strategies are to be used within a given medium to solicit attention. Since both the number of media and the available strategies are restricted, there necessarily arise parallels and superimpositions—but also delimitations, adaptations, and distortions—between the forms of intervention employed in diverse social realms (politics, culture, advertising, etc.).

While this process of reciprocal conditioning is observable in all media, it is especially conspicuous in the case of the poster, whose potential for conveying information is restricted by its necessary orientation toward simple legibility. The enormous "coverage" of the poster in so-called public space results from the circumstance that although passers-by are more or less unavoidably confronted by their messages (i.e. depending upon placement), such contact does not necessarily generate heightened attentiveness. As a consequence, the poster medium requires striking, memorable designs involving text and visual information—and moreover regardless of whether the purpose is to market commodities, win support for a political party, or mount an appeal for social action. In this context, design is interesting less in terms of aesthetic categories and more as a representational system which engenders intrinsic relationships between visuality, legality, identity, economy, and power, one that poses questions related to cultural, social, economic, and political motivations and strategies.

Dramatically present, at least since the 1980s, have been the questions, the anxieties, and the calls for action in the realms of private enterprise, the political sphere, and individual life, all of them propelled by such phenomena as the entry of the Greens into the European Parliament; the dawning awareness of dying forests and Chernobyl; a second wave of mass tourism; an inexorable globalization which seeks to justify its market and economic effects; the rise of nongovernmental development programs; the first conferences on climate; and unemployment levels that have not been discussed in the context of labor migration. In search of social and political action, such at-times striking, at-times helpless messages, with their appeals to solidarity, penetrated the nurseries of an entire generation, anchoring themselves in the consciousness of everyday life: "Save the Trees," "Make Peace Not War," "Nuclear Power? No Thanks!"; suspended above our beds on posters and stickers were these and similar slogans, trophies of an awareness of social injustice and the necessity for a reorientation of thinking.

Such slogans were designed to motivate, to oppose subliminal anxieties concerning the future with positive action, to establish solidarity, and to induce a sense of bad conscience. Such appeals and their accompanying rhetoric are produced and exploited by both state-sponsored and non-governmental initiatives. Strikingly, very few deploy a subversive, nuanced textual and image language. Instead, it was and remains a question of reaching the collective consciousness. But the question remains: Who speaks, and why, and how, and to whom?

Since the 1980s, the social appeals found in posters have mirrored a history, one that tells us much concerning political debates, their participants and protagonists, and their respective languages. But of special interest beyond this is the question of how we are addressed, of the manner in which the perspectives of speaker and receiver are constructed, displaced, unmasked, or reversed. A one-sided sender/ receiver communication model is here disrupted in favor of the priority of questions of experiences of identity and difference among both receivers and producers.

Postcolonial studies (in dialogue with gender and psychoanalytic studies) has investigated hybrid structures of identity and questions concerning translation with reference to experiences of difference and of various "others." In this context, experiences of difference are no longer sought in the "outside" or the "other," but are instead redefined in terms of one's own consciousness. In *Strangers to Ourselves,*[2] for instance, Julia Kristeva formulates this experience of difference as an intersubjective structure, one which defines the "other" as the unconscious of the self. An entire series of poster initiatives have deconstructed the received identitarian myth, calling attention to the "foreigner within ourselves."

Announced, for example, in the form of an obituary in a 1994 Greenpeace campaign poster is the self-accusation: "I ruin the climate, because my power plants spew 100,000,000 tons of CO_2 into the atmosphere annually." Pictured is Dr. Dietmar Kuhnt, chairman of RWE Energie AG. Greenpeace here articulates a subjective appeal by the individual to his/her conscience or unconscious, giving public expression to the unspoken, the silent. In a poster campaign by the initiative Anschläge.de in the framework of the series "Hier spricht Barmbek.Barmbek.TV" (Barmbek speaks here! Barmbek.TV), Paula—a retiree—asks in the name of her suffering fellow elderly: "Honestly, could you survive on 100 € per month?" 72 She demands that poverty among the elderly be confronted as a problem affecting one's own neighbors, not passed over in embarrassed silence as a problem of isolated individuals. The artist's posters of Roland Piltz and Aisha Ronniger pursue a different strategy: by montaging various (also gender-connoted) details of portraits and text fragments ("New York / Vladimir / Unemployed") in a silkscreening process, they contradict superficial identitarian notions of the construction of the subject. 83 Some details offer possibilities for identification; others do not, leading to an interrogation of phantasms of identification.

Colonial practices continue to persist, as described among others by Kien Nghi Ha in his book *Ethnizität und Migration* (Ethnicity and migration).[3] Despite formal independence from the European powers, the colonial gaze and power constellations perpetuate and reproduce themselves by structuring social relations. The same is true of some poster campaigns, and is especially clear regarding questions of global mobility: one group is said to "migrate," the other to "travel." In one design, Klaus Staeck responds to this schizophrenia with the following slogan: "During each vacation season, millions of Germans become foreigners" 114. A "white" couple is set alone against the South Sea backdrop. Their stencil-style silhouettes are reinforced by the text, for they appear to have been simply collaged into the scene, joined not to the larger context, but only with one another. From a different perspective, this absence of exchange or mutual involvement thematizes processes of segregation in German cities or urban peripheries, as for example in Gunter Rambow's poster "Deutschland den Deutschen," whose German text translates as: "German for the Germans / Frankfurt for the Frankfurters / Seckbach for the Seckbachers / Herr Meier for Herr Meier / Racism Makes Us Lonely" 76. The five lines of red text are set like prison bars in front of the portrayed individual, presumably having a foreign background. Conveyed via the sequence "Germany, Frankfurt, Seckbach" is a progression that concludes with "Herr Meier," representative of the many "Herr Meiers" who condemn themselves to loneliness via exclusive and restrictive social behavior, ultimately positioning themselves, figuratively speaking, behind prison bars of their own making. A recurring topos in posters dealing with identity and ethnicity is the loneliness engendered by fear—whether on the part of tourists, immigrants, or nationalists.

An additional strategy raising awareness of the continuing impact of the matrix of colonial history and triggering self-reflection concerning subjective knowledge perspectives is the reversal of speaker standpoints: a poster by Meta-Cultura, Zurich, shows a mural of the Hima in Uganda in combination with the statement "White men think too much" by "a village chief from Mali" (a reference to the title of a legendary book by Paul Parin, Fritz Morgenthaler, and Goldy Parin-Matthèy).[4] 94 The poster, commissioned by Helvetas, a Swiss society for development and cooperation, is irritating in several respects: beneath the statement by the village chief, we read: "Indigenous peoples have much to tell us. In the Helvetas special volume *Ureinwohner* [Indigenous Peoples], they have their say." Whether consciously or unconsciously, the use of the term "indigenous peoples" simultaneously romanticizes, archaizes, and exoticizes the knowledge context of the "village chief." The initially provocative reversal of perspectives is threatened by loss of credibility, of becoming pedantic. Something similar occurs in a poster campaign by Swissaid: "Spielen Sie Wilhelm Tell" (Do like William Tell) 120. The visual adaptation of the William Tell gesture, one intended to remind Swiss citizens of their own mythic liberation and national identity, enjoins viewers to liberate themselves by shooting a mango or pineapple with a bow and arrow. The scene there is the subtitle: "Donate freedom. Help that helps people help themselves." Help for self-help, one that has become—thanks to Friedrich Schiller's drama of 1804—a "Helvetic activity." But does the idea of help for self-help not reveal itself here rhetorically as meaning "Do as we do?" Or does the campaign instead lead to an incapacity for action—even if we assume that the Tell campaign is ironically intended, that it questions itself reflexively?

A different approach is taken by the Stiftung Gegen Rassismus und Antisemitismus (Foundation Against Racism and Anti-Semitism): "Where do Kosovo Albanians get their car radios? At a store, like most Swiss people." 116 Or: "What do Thai women do when it gets dark? Turn on the lights, like most Swiss people." 118 This game of question and answer is so simpleminded, the pictorial wisecracks so comic book or fairytale-like, it is difficult not to smile. At the same time, they are reminiscent of jokes that begin: "What do the Chinese do when…?" Both on the textual and image levels, these designs have recourse to familiar codes, albeit now subversively modified. Roland Barthes once asked: "Is not the best subversion the one which distorts the codes instead of destroying them?"[5] This idea was available to many artistic groups, for example communication or prankster guerrillas engaging in actions and medial interventions that attempt in a subversive spirit to endow medial, visual, or textual languages with new meanings.

Interestingly, very few initiatives take advantage of subversive strategies. Invoked instead is a kind of self-discipline, a governmental mode of discourse that appeals to the subject and demands political rationality. One example of this is Woody Pirtle, whose poster series appeals to the collective consciousness and reminds us of human rights by citing Article 25 of the "Universal Declaration of Human Rights," which states that "Everyone Has the Right to an Adequate Standard of Living" 22. Others, on the other hand, gesture toward a purely economic logic, for instance a poster by Ogilvy & Mather AG, Zurich: appearing above an image of a full glass of beer are the words, "Enough to provide a child in Haiti with hot meals for a month / Caritas / Need has many faces. Donation account 60-700-4" 119.

When it comes to social causes, the degree of conventionality and seriousness of both text and image rises proportionally to the "gravity" of the topic involved—in contrast to commercial advertising, which promises us happiness, wealth, beauty, etc., through our participation in the prestige associated with the image of the marketed product, and which often makes no attempt to reflect reality. This mechanism reflects the unspoken distinction between commercial advertising and cultural and political discourse. This distinction presupposes a media competency, the assumption that as a rule, no one will confuse the promises proffered by advertising with reality, while the statements and appeals made by NGOs and other initiatives are expected to be based on a concrete sense of realism. The firmness of this boundary line is best perceived by considering a case in which this unspoken contract has been violated.

By far the most prominent instance in this context is the ad campaign developed by the photographer Oliviero Toscani for the fashion firm Benetton, one that earned worldwide attention see pp. 64–67. The firm insisted that the advertisements were designed to provoke an awareness of social responsibility, that the campaign was intended less to market its products and more to call attention to political issues, taboos, and social grievances. Critics, however, regarded it as unethical to exploit human suffering to increase profit margins. The controversy points up the way in which the Benetton campaign, with its striking display of images of war 101, HIV/ AIDS 100, death, racism 97, environmental degradation 57, death row inmates 73, 75, the suffering of refugees 2, etc., had evidently transgressed unspoken boundaries. The same images displayed routinely in news broadcasts—for example the one of the oil-drenched duck swimming in an oil slick 57—were simply unacceptable in the context of an advertising campaign.

The complexity of any attempt to assess this campaign is suggested by the circumstance that, on the one hand, it triggered protests and legal actions, while on the other being taken up in some countries in the context of AIDS consciousness-raising and anti-racism campaigns. Needless to add, they were also collected and exhibited among the poster collections of many museums. From the perspective of the economy of attention, certainly, the campaign was a resounding success: it transformed an Italian knitwear firm into one of the best-known labels worldwide.

With regard to the social appeal of the poster as a medium, the question formulated at the beginning of this essay, "Who Appeals to Whom, and How, and to What Ends?" is necessary if we are to determine by what motivations and strategies specific textual and visual idioms are placed in the foreground, who is addressed by them, and by whom. Strategies which thematize the perspective of the sender, and subversive or exaggeratedly affirmative statements, provide insights going behind the striking surfaces of these images, making possible a closer examination of the motivations and intentions of poster designers and their clients.

1 Georg Franck, *Ökonomie der Aufmerksamkeit. Ein Entwurf* (Munich and Vienna 1998).
2 Julia Kristeva, *Strangers to Ourselves* (New York et al. 1994).
3 Kien Nghi Ha, *Ethnizität und Migration* (Münster 1999).
4 Paul Parin et al., *Die Weissen denken zuviel. Psychoanalytische Untersuchungen bei den Dogon in Westafrika* (Zurich 1963).
5 Roland Barthes, *Sade-Fourier-Loyola* (Berkeley 1989).

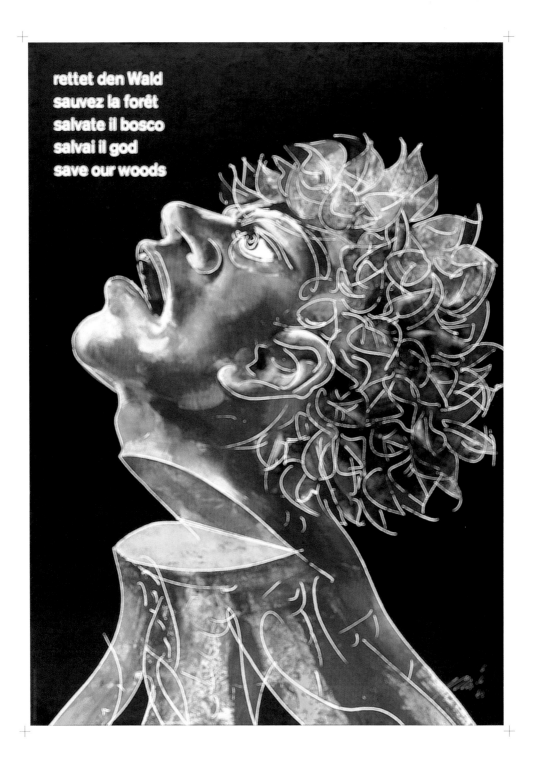

rettet den Wald
sauvez la forêt
salvate il bosco
salvai il god
save our woods

44 **Hans Erni**
Rettet den Wald / Aktion «Rettet den Wald»
1983 CH

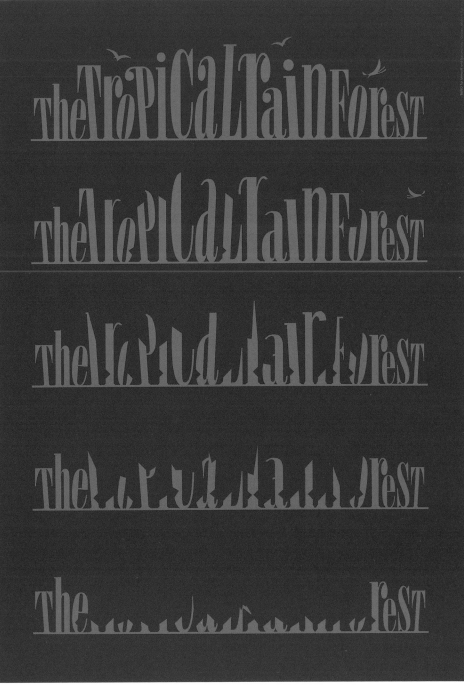

45 **Andreas Karl**
The tropical rain forest / Bund für Umwelt
und Naturschutz Deutschland
1995 DE

STOP DEFORESTATION / SÉBASTIEN COURTOIS FABRICATION MAISON 2005

46 **Sébastien Courtois**
Stop deforestation
2005 FR

47 **Anonym**
Chaque mois disparaît dans le monde l'équivalent
de la forêt suisse…/Direction de la Coopération au
développement et de l'aide humanitaire, 1983 CH

48 **U. G. Sato**
I'm here./Japan Graphic Designers Association, 1993 JP

49 **Select International**
3 Euro retten seine Welt./World Wildlife Fund
2008 DE

50 **Savaş Çekiç**
Stil Matbaasi
1998 TR

*W*here
can
Nature
go?

51 **U. G. Sato**
Where can Nature go?
1993 JP

52 **Niklaus Troxler**
1992 CH

53 **Savaş Çekiç**
Stil Matbaasi
1998 TR

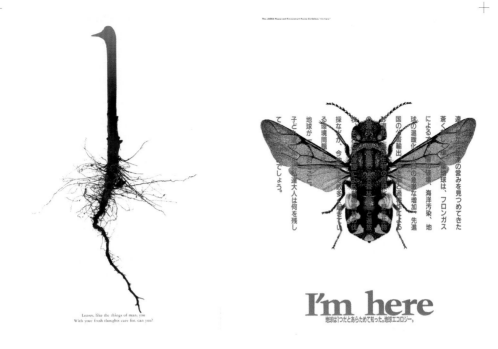

Leaves, like the things of man, you
With your fresh thoughts care for, can you?

地球は1つだとあらためて知った。地球エコロジー。

Спасти хочу земную красоту...
А.С.Пушкин

54 **Masuteru Aoba**
Leaves, like the things of man, you / Japan
Graphic Designers Association, 1992 JP

55 **Sergej Kužavski**
Spasti choču zemnuju krasotu... – A.S. Puškin /
World Wildlife Fund, ca. 1995 RU

56 **Tomoko Inue / Masato Watanabe**
I'm here / Japan Graphic Designers Association
ca. 1993 JP

57 **Oliviero Toscani**
United Colors of Benetton. / Benetton Group S.p.A.
1992 IT

58 **Publicis Werbeagentur AG**
Warum auch Fische Ferien brauchen. /
Migros-Genossenschafts-Bund, 2006 CH

Beach Party

Klimaveränderung – wann werden wir aus Schaden klug?

Whirl Pool

Stopp der Klimaveränderung!

Kreuzfahrt

Verändern Sie sich, damit sich das Klima nicht verändert.

59 **Hochschule für Gestaltung und Kunst Luzern**
Beach Party / Stadt Luzern Umweltschutz
1995 CH

60 **Hochschule für Gestaltung und Kunst Luzern**
Kreuzfahrt / Stadt Luzern Umweltschutz
1995 CH

61 **Hochschule für Gestaltung und Kunst Luzern**
Whirl Pool / Stadt Luzern Umweltschutz
1995 CH

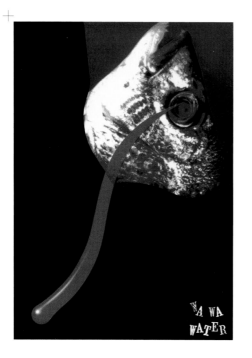

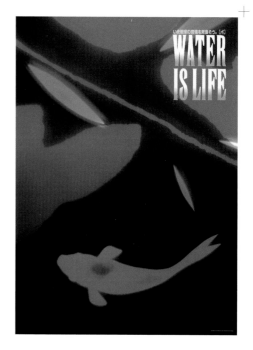

62 **Kiyotaka Hotta**
Wa Wa Water / Japan Graphic Designers Association
1991 JP

63 **Surič Design**
Water for human kind. / L'association pour une banque
d'images: L'eau pour l'humanité, 2000 RU

64 **Takahiro Shima**
Water is life / Japan Graphic Designers Association
1990 JP

65 **James Victore**
Earth Day
1995 US

Save The Water

66 **Naoki Hirai**
Save The Water
2002 JP

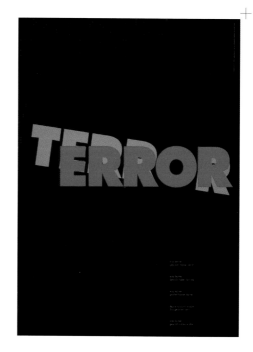

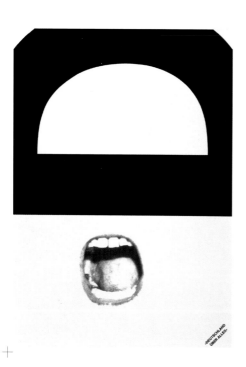

67 **Gerda Frisch**
AI hilft gewaltlosen politischen Gefangenen in aller
Welt / Amnesty International, ca. 1985 DE

68 **Ralph Schraivogel**
«Deutschland über Alles» / Allianz Deutscher Designer
et al., 1993 CH

69 **Germar Wambach**
Terror Error / Allianz Deutscher Designer et al.
1992 DE

70 **Claude Baillargeon**
SOS Injustices / Mairie de Bagnolet
1990 FR

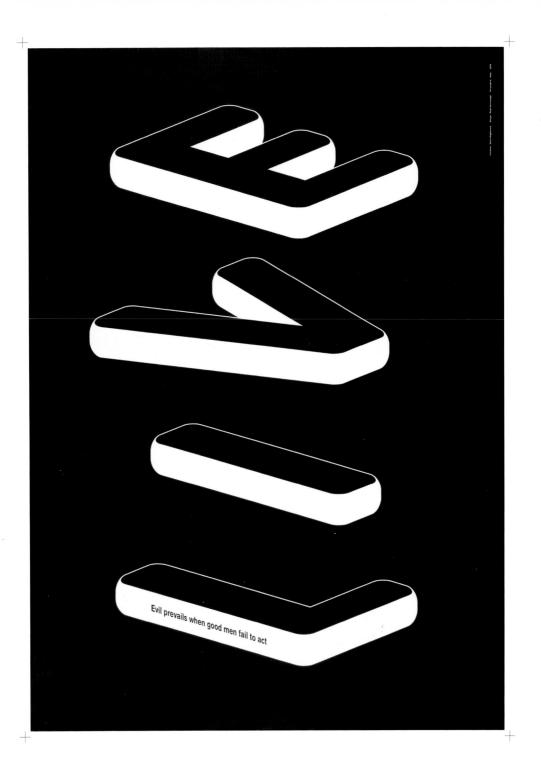

Evil prevails when good men fail to act

71 **Ralph Schraivogel**
Live – Evil / Sacha Wigdorovits
2009 CH

72 **anschlaege.de**
«Mal ganz ehrlich, können Sie mit 100 Euro im Monat
auskommen?» / Kampnagel, Internationale Kulturfabrik
GmbH, 2007 DE

73 **Oliviero Toscani**
Zum Tode verurteilt / Benetton Group S.p.A., 2000 IT

74 **anschlaege.de**
«Jeder wird ernten, was er sät. Wird er Liebe säen,
wird er auch Liebe ernten.» / Kampnagel, Internationale
Kulturfabrik GmbH, 2007 DE

75 **Oliviero Toscani**
Zum Tode verurteilt / Benetton Group S.p.A., 2000 IT

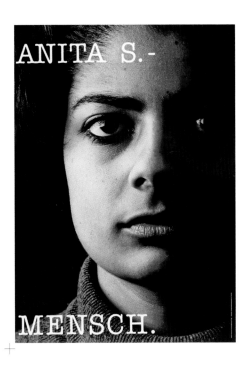

76 **Gunter Rambow**
Deutschland den Deutschen / Deutscher
Gewerkschaftsbund et al., 1995 DE

77 **Andreas Fechner / Bernward Kraft**
Anita S. – Mensch. / Allianz Deutscher Designer
et al., 1993 DE

78 **Gunter Rambow**
Deutschland den Deutschen / Deutscher
Gewerkschaftsbund et al., 1995 DE

79 **Andreas Fechner / Bernward Kraft**
Tom D. – Mensch. / Allianz Deutscher Designer
et al., 1993 DE

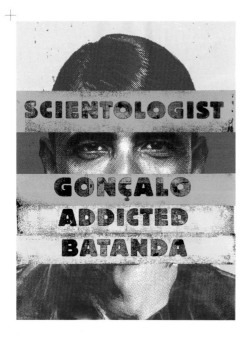

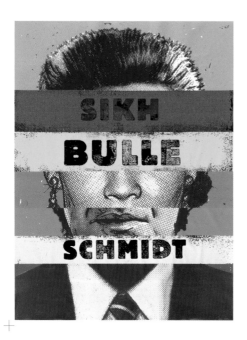

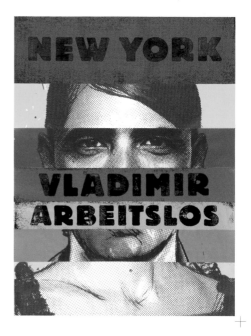

80 **Roland Piltz / Aisha Ronniger**
Scientologist – Gonçalo – Addicted – Batanda /
Kunsthochschule Berlin Weissensee, 2007 DE

81 **Roland Piltz / Aisha Ronniger**
Sikh – Bulle – Schmidt / Kunsthochschule Berlin
Weissensee, 2007 DE

82 **Roland Piltz / Aisha Ronniger**
Istanbul – Hero – Parvati – Sarajevo / Kunsthochschule
Berlin Weissensee, 2007 DE

83 **Roland Piltz / Aisha Ronniger**
New York – Vladimir – Arbeitslos / Kunsthochschule
Berlin Weissensee, 2007 DE

84 **Urs Grünig**
Menschenrechte für Alle / Amnesty International
1999 CH

Racism and the Death Penalty

85 **James Victore**
Racism and the Death Penalty / Legal Defense
and Educational Fund / American Civil Liberties Union
1993 US

86 **James Victore**
Racism, 1993 US

87 **James Victore**
Hate / Anti-Defamation League of New York
1997 US

The Death Penalty Mocks Justice

The United States remains the only Western industrialized nation to retain the death penalty and carry out executions. While the rest of the world turns its back on state sanctioned killing, the death penalty in the U.S. continues to be applied in a racist and arbitrary manner. Capital punishment has never been implemented in a fair and non-discriminatory way. It has never been proven to be a deterrent, yet our nations death row, and executions continue to escalate. The death penalty is a mockery of justice. In the pursuit of equality before the law it must be abolished.

88 **James Victore**
The Death Penalty Mocks Justice /
Legal Defense and Educational Fund
1995 US

89 **Eva Kemény / László Sós**
Ministry of Environment and Water Supply
1988 HU

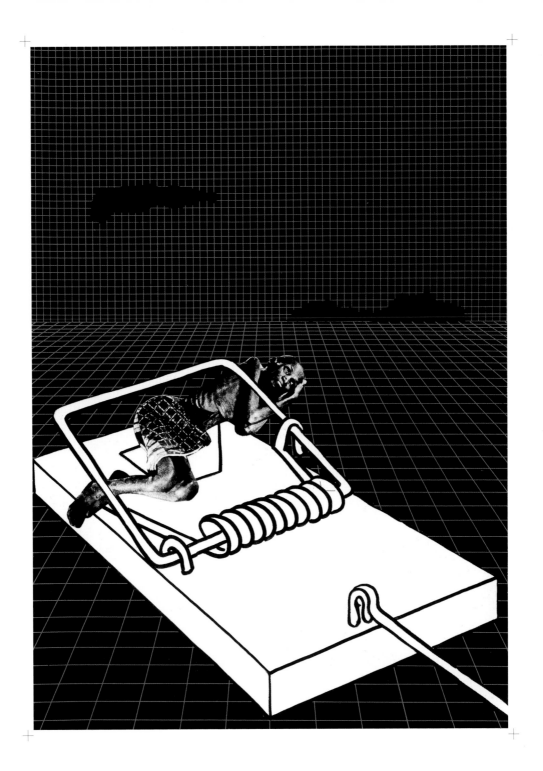

90 **Eva Kemény / László Sós**
Ministry of Environment and Water Supply
1988 HU

MOST STATES WOULD HAVE PUT THESE KIDS IN REFORM SCHOOL. VIRGINIA PUT THEM TO DEATH.

Clem Cive and Bill James are just two of the 29 children who have been executed in Virginia. Let's change the laws that allow this to happen. Call Amnesty International USA if you'd like to know how to help. **AMNESTY INTERNATIONAL USA. 1-800-55AMNESTY**

MAYBE THE DEATH PENALTY SHOULD HAVE BEEN ELIMINATED A LONG TIME AGO.

Every time the state kills, it affects each one of us. Let's stop it. Call Amnesty International USA if you'd like to know how to help. **AMNESTY INTERNATIONAL USA. 1-800-55AMNESTY**

91 **Jerry Torchia**
Most states would have put these kids
in reform school. / Amnesty International
1992 US

92 **Jerry Torchia**
Maybe the death penalty should have been eliminated
a long time ago. / Amnesty International
1992 US

Stoppt die Folter.

amnesty international
Kampagne gegen die Folter
Spendenkonto 30-3417 **ai**

93 **Stephan Bundi**
Stoppt die Folter. / Amnesty International
1985 CH

Wandbemalung der Hima, Uganda

"Die Weissen denken zuviel"

Ein Dorfchef aus Mali

Ureinwohner haben uns viel zu sagen. Im Helvetas Spezialheft "Ureinwohner"
kommen sie zu Wort. Bestellen Sie kostenlos ein Exemplar. Telefon 01 / 363 37 56

Helvetas, Schweizer Gesellschaft für Entwicklung und Zusammenarbeit
St. Moritzstrasse 15, 8042 Zürich

94 **Meta-Cultura**
«Die Weissen denken zuviel» / Helvetas
1993 CH

95 **Vladimir Antonov**
Amnesty International
1993

ZEITGENÖSSISCHE «BILDERSTÜRMER»

«Solche Bilder können nicht mehr sein als eine Aufforderung zur Aufmerksamkeit, zum Nachdenken, zum Lernen – dazu, die Rationalisierung für massenhaftes Leiden, die von den etablierten Mächten angeboten werden, kritisch zu prüfen. Wer hat das, was auf dem Bild zu sehen ist, verursacht? Wer ist verantwortlich? Ist es entschuldbar? War es unvermeidlich? Haben wir eine bestimmte Situation bisher fraglos akzeptiert, die in Frage gestellt werden sollte? Dies alles – und obendrein die Einsicht, dass weder moralische Empörung noch Mitgefühl das Handeln bestimmen können.»
Susan Sontag[1]

Originalität, Neuartigkeit, kommunikative Nachhaltigkeit: Dies sind nur einige der Schlagworte aus dem Handbuch erfolgreichen PR-Managements. Die Resultate hingegen, die uns täglich auf Werbeflächen begegnen, enttäuschen jede Erwartung. Affirmation und Konformismus prägen den medialen Auftritt im öffentlichen Raum. Selbst kulturelle und soziale Plakate folgen immer mehr den konditionierten Bahnen der Konsumwerbung. Dass das Plakat trotz seiner grossen Verbreitung kaum als Chance zur Innovation und Provokation genutzt wird, muss immerhin erstaunen.

WERBEN MIT GEWALT

Der Fotograf Oliviero Toscani hat mit seinen polarisierenden Benetton-Kampagnen aus den Jahren 1983 bis 2000 vorgeführt, dass es selbst im Bereich der kommerziellen Werbung durchaus möglich ist, mit einer neuen Bildrhetorik Aufmerksamkeit zu erzielen. Wenngleich mittlerweile etwas desillusioniert, fordert er noch heute, die immensen Werbebudgets zu nutzen, um dringliche soziale und politische Fragen zu thematisieren. Den meisten Werbern attestiert er diesbezüglich nicht nur fehlenden Mut, sondern auch Verrat an Intelligenz und Kreativität.

Toscanis Plakate für Benetton illustrieren seine eigene Entwicklung und Radikalisierung. Die frühen Arbeiten zeigen fotografische Variationen einer Welt, die Schwarz, Weiss und Gelb vereint. Mögen solche multikulturellen Botschaften heute schon fast zum guten Ton gehören, so rüttelten diese Bilder in den 1980er Jahren am Selbstverständnis des Publikums und stellten Rollenklischees infrage. 1993 begann Toscani damit, ausgewählte Reportagefotos im Grossformat zu zeigen. «Zum ersten Mal nutzte die Werbung ein paar Quadratmeter ihrer gigantischen Fläche, um der Öffentlichkeit Aktualität in ihren extremen Bildern zu vermitteln, mit einer Schlagkraft, die tausendmal stärker war als die aller Nachrichtenmagazine zusammen.»[2]

Die unerwartete und unausweichliche Konfrontation mit diesen Bildern im urbanen Raum, die sich nicht einfach wegblättern oder wegzappen liessen, musste provozieren. Der heftige Vorwurf an Toscani auch seitens Berufskollegen, das eigentliche Ziel der Werbung misszuverstehen und das Moralempfinden zu verletzen, ist allerdings verräterisch. Meint dies doch, dass der Werbung einzig die Aufgabe zukommt, heuchlerische Bilder einer heilen Welt zu streuen, Stereotypen zu untermauern und die Passanten vor Herausforderungen und «Zumutungen» jeder Art zu schützen.

Dass Luciano Benetton, der gemeinsam mit Toscani die Marketing-Strategie des Unternehmens entwickelte, aus reinem Profitstreben zynisch das Leid von Menschen ausbeutet, widerlegt die 1994 gegründete Fabrica. Ziel dieses Forschungszentrums für Kommunikation ist es, internationale Künstler und Designer in einem kreativen think tank zu vereinen und die Kommunikation nach neuen, ethisch vertretbaren Wegen zu befragen. Wieso sollte es nicht legitim sein, Unternehmertum und soziale Verantwortung mittels der Werbung zu verbinden? Eine Frage, die es umso mehr heute zu stellen gilt, da *Corporate Social Responsibility* zwar in aller Munde ist, sich jedoch kaum öffentlich manifestiert.

Die Zusammenarbeit zwischen Luciano Benetton und Oliviero Toscani endete schliesslich mit einem schweren Zerwürfnis. Toscanis Appell gegen die Todesstrafe, mit Porträts von Todeskandidaten aus US-Gefängnissen visuell eindringlich vermittelt, führte zu so heftigen Kontroversen, dass Benetton den Vertrag mit ihm kündigte. Obwohl Toscani heute darauf beharrt, dass es im Unternehmertum einzig um wirtschaftliche Gewinninteressen geht und auch Benetton nie andere Ziele verfolgte, ist er seinen Strategien – nicht ganz widerspruchsfrei – doch treu geblieben. Dies belegt sein Plakat von 2007 für das italienische Modelabel Nolita mit einem magersüchtigen Model, das einmal mehr leidenschaftliche Diskussionen auslöste und in Italien verboten und abmontiert wurde.

Es ist Toscanis und Benettons Verdienst, grundlegende Diskussionen über Sinn, Zweck und Möglichkeiten der Werbung angeregt zu haben. Dennoch bleibt ein Unbehagen, weiss man um den kommerziellen Auftraggeber und kennt die Benetton-Philosophie nicht weiter. Geht es tatsächlich um mehr als um Aufmerksamkeitsgenerierung? Und mit dieser Frage kann man sich als Adressat auch selbst wieder der Verantwortung entledigen. Ein sozialer Absender hingegen vermittelt eine andere Glaubwürdigkeit, allerdings exponieren sich entwicklungspolitische Organisationen selten mit solchen ausgezeichneten, realitätsnahen Bildern.

MIT KAMERUN AUF AUGENHÖHE

Michael von Graffenrieds grossformatige Fotografien aus Kamerun, die gedruckt und auf öffentlichen Plakatwänden gezeigt wurden, veranschaulichen beispielhaft, welche Rolle der Auftraggeber für die Rezeption spielt. Während Toscani letztlich als gewiefter PR-Stratege gilt, der mit durchaus ethischen Absichten für einen finanzkräftigen Modekonzern operiert, interveniert Graffenried als engagierter Künstler und Fotograf im städtischen Raum. Daher muss er auch keine Kompromisse eingehen: Kein Gewinn muss erzielt, kein Spendenerfolg nachgewiesen, auch kein Skandal provoziert werden. Sein jüngster Zyklus, «eye on africa»[3], entstand in Zusammenarbeit mit Fairmed zum 50-jährigen Jubiläum der Organisation, jedoch bewusst nicht als Plakatkampagne für Fairmed. Die Panoramabilder wurden im Format 125 x 270 cm im März 2009 in fünf Schweizer Städten auf öffentlichen Werbeflächen gehängt, zugleich als Serie vor dem Zentrum Paul Klee in Bern ausgestellt.

Geht es Toscani bei der Wahl der Bilder wesentlich darum aufzurütteln, ist von Graffenrieds Blick – und damit auch seine Absicht – unspektakulärer und stiller. Die

Dramatik der Bilder, mit denen Toscani auf humane und ökologische Katastrophen verweist – man denke an das christomorphe Porträt des Aidskranken im Kreis seiner Familie – fehlt bei Graffenried. Beim Betrachten seiner Panoramafotografien, die Menschen verschiedener sozialer Klassen bei ihren alltäglichen Beschäftigungen zeigen, funktioniert keine schockartige – oftmals aber auch nur kurzlebige Betroffenheit. Die Perspektive ist so gewählt, dass der Passant in die Szenerie hineingezogen wird. Anlässlich einer Ausstellung im Jahr 2003, die Fotografien Graffenrieds aus der Schweiz und Algerien gegenüberstellte, schrieb Harald Szeemann: «Beide Welten geben sich dem Betrachter auf Augenhöhe, werden also zu objektiven Bildwelten ohne die Dramatisierung über diverse Blickpunkte, versuchen also den (Kunst-)Betrachter direkt ins Bildgeschehen einzubeziehen.»[4]

Bei Graffenried begegnen uns Individuen, die zum Dialog einladen. Und dieser Dialog ist ein ebenbürtiger, der nicht vorschnell klischierte Rollenbilder von privilegiert und unterprivilegiert, vertraut und exotisch bestätigt. Diese Gleichwertigkeit im Blick auf eine andere Kultur, aus der stets der Respekt des Fotografen spricht, vermittelt sich auch den Betrachtern. Neugier und Offenheit gegenüber dem Fremden statt Mitleid und Arroganz bestimmen damit die Wahrnehmung.

Auf ihre je eigene Weise und in ganz unterschiedlichem Kontext nutzen Toscani und Graffenried den öffentlichen Raum, um der Abgeschmacktheit der Werbung eine andere Sicht gegenüberzustellen. Dabei nehmen sie ihr Publikum ernst, fordern es heraus, laden zu einem neuen Blick ein. Sie agieren als zeitgenössische «Bilderstürmer», die entscheidende Fragen aufwerfen und so dem durch die Konsumwerbung vermittelten eindimensionalen Weltbild begegnen und zu neuen Auseinandersetzungen anregen.

Bettina Richter

96 **Oliviero Toscani**
United Colors of Benetton. / Benetton Group S.p.A.
1992 IT

«In meiner Werbung möchte ich mit der Öffentlichkeit über die Macht des Klischees und über Gemeinplätze kommunizieren (schliesslich ist die Werbung voll davon). Über Fügsamkeit und Freiheit des Geistes. Über Toleranz. Warum verharren bloss die meisten in ihrer ersten Reaktion, der rassistischen oder antirassistischen Tabuisierung? Warum sollte die Werbung nicht, wie die Kunst oder die Medien, eine Spielwiese der Philosophie, ein Emotionskatalysator, ein Forum für Streit und Polemik sein? Ich war zweifellos derjenige, der von den gewaltigen Reaktionen und von der Kraft des rassistischen Klischees am meisten überrascht wurde. Daraufhin erkannte ich aber, dass das Spiel mit Stereotypen eine grossartige Möglichkeit bietet, mit anerzogenen und hingenommenen Meinungen aufzuräumen.»
Oliviero Toscani, 1995

Zitiert nach: Oliviero Toscani, Die Werbung ist ein lächelndes Aas, Mannheim 1996. Franz. Erstausgabe: La Pub est une charogne qui nous sourit, Paris 1995.

«Bei meinen Fotografien geht es immer darum, Menschen einander vorzustellen, die sich unter natürlichen Umständen nie begegnen würden. Um diese Begegnungen zu ermöglichen, suche ich Menschen, die ich in authentischen Situationen ablichte. Danach bringe ich die Bilder in eine neue Umgebung, in der dann der Betrachter mit diesen Menschen konfrontiert wird. Dies ist auch der Grund, weshalb die Bilder so gross (als Plakate, Anm. Hrsg.) gezeigt werden. Der Betrachter fühlt sich ins Bild reingezogen und meint, er sei zusammen mit diesen Menschen dort. Bei ‹eye on africa› geht es darum, solche Begegnungen zu schaffen. Der Betrachter in der Schweiz lässt sich auf die Menschen aus Afrika auf dem Bildpanorama ein und kann so vielleicht ein wenig die Distanz zum Fremden abbauen. ‹eye on africa› zeigt die Vielfalt und Schönheit des afrikanischen Kontinents und steht im Kontrast zur Gewalt und Armut, die wir seit langem mit diesem Kontinent assoziieren. Weiter unterstreicht für mich der Umstand, dass in den Vereinigten Staaten von Amerika im Jahr 2009 ein Afroamerikaner das Amt des Präsidenten inne hält, diesen erfreulichen Trend klar.»
Michael von Graffenried, 2009.

*Zitiert nach
www.fairmed.ch/50/dl/mvg_interview_lang_d.pdf*

1 Susan Sontag, *Das Leiden anderer betrachten*, München/Wien 2003, S. 236.
2 Oliviero Toscani, *Die Werbung ist ein lächelndes Aas*, Mannheim 1996, S. 56.
3 Michael von Graffenried, *Michael von Graffenried: eye on africa. Fotografien aus Kamerun / Photographies du Cameroun / Photographs from Cameroon*, Basel 2009.
4 Harald Szeemann, «Einführung», in: Kunstmuseum Bern, *Zwischen Welten = Entre deux mondes: Michael von Graffenried*, Bern 2003.

97 **Oliviero Toscani**
United Colors of
Benetton. / Benetton
Group S.p.A.
1989 IT

98 **Oliviero Toscani**
United Colors of
Benetton. / Benetton
Group S.p.A.
1991 IT

99 **Oliviero Toscani**
United Colors of
Benetton. / Benetton
Group S.p.A.
1992 IT

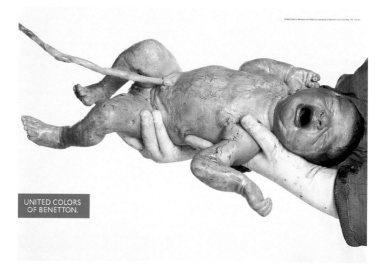

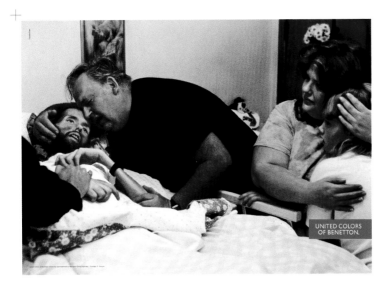

100 **Oliviero Toscani**
United Colors of
Benetton. / Benetton
Group S.p.A.
1992 IT

101 **Oliviero Toscani**
United Colors of
Benetton. / Benetton
Group S.p.A.
1991 IT

102 **Oliviero Toscani**
United Colors of
Benetton.
White – Black – Yellow /
Benetton Group S.p.A.
1996 IT

103–112 **Atelier Gerhard**
Blättler / Michael
von Graffenried
2009 CH
[Kamerun – Cameroon, 2008]

69

CONTEMPORARY «ICONOCLASTS»

Photographic images from wars cannot be more than an invitation to pay attention, to reflect, to learn, to examine the rationalisation for mass suffering offered by established powers. Who caused the images that the picture shows? Who is responsible? Is it excusable? Was it inevitable? Is there some state of affairs which we have accepted up to now that ought to be challenged? All this and the understanding that moral indignation, like compassion, cannot dictate a course of action.
Susan Sontag[1]

Originality, novelty, communicative sustainability: these are just a few slogans found in handbooks on successful PR management. And yet the results we encounter daily in advertising contexts disappoint all of our expectations. Medial images found in the public realm are conditioned by affirmation and conformism. Even posters conveying cultural and social messages consistently follow the predictable channels of consumer advertising. Consistently astonishing is the reality that despite its vast diffusion, the poster is rarely exploited as an opportunity for innovation or provocation.

FORCEFUL SOLICITATION

With his polarizing Benetton campaign dating from 1983 to 2000, photographer Oliviero Toscani demonstrated that even in the realm of commercial advertising it is possible to attract considerable attention through a new visual rhetoric. Despite having become somewhat disillusioned in the meantime, he still calls for using a portion of the immense commercial advertising budgets to thematize urgent social and political questions. In this regard, he charges the majority of advertisers not just with cowardice, but also with a betrayal of intelligence and creativity.

Toscani's posters for Benetton illustrate his own development and his gradual radicalization. The early works displayed photographic images of a world where black, white, and yellow were united. And although such multicultural messages are today regarded as virtually obligatory, in the 1980s his photographs still rubbed public sensibilities the wrong way, calling stereotypical clichés into question. In 1993, Toscani began exhibiting selected reportage photographs in large format. "For the first time, advertising used a few square meters of its gigantic surface area to convey reality to the public in extreme images which had an impact a thousand times greater than all news magazines combined."[2]

Unexpected and unavoidable confrontations in urban spaces with these images–which could not be evaded by turning the page or switching channels–were necessarily provocative. The vigorous objections directed at Toscani by professional colleagues, and according to whom he misunderstood the real objectives of advertising and offended moral sensibilities, were certainly traitorous. According to them, the sole task of advertising was to disseminate duplicitous images of an ideal world, reinforcing stereotypes and sparing passers-by challenges or "impositions" of any kind.

The notion that Luciano Benetton, who developed his enterprise's marketing strategy jointly with Toscani, cynically exploited human suffering in his quest for profits is refuted by the Fabrica, founded in 1994. The objective of this research center for communication is to bring together international artists and designers in a creative think tank to investigate new, ethically defensible paths. Why should it not be regarded as legitimate to connect entrepreneurship and social responsibility via advertising? The question is all the more relevant today, with so much talk about a "corporate social responsibility" that is so rarely actually in evidence.

In the end, the collaboration between Luciano Benetton and Oliviero Toscani ended in sharp discord. Toscani's appeal to end the death penalty, conveyed strikingly through portraits of death row inmates in US prisons, led to such contentiousness that Benetton canceled his contract. Although Toscani today insists that commercial enterprises are concerned solely with their own economic interests, and that Benetton never pursued any other objectives, he has nonetheless remained true to his strategy–if not entirely without self-contradiction. This is illustrated by his 2007 poster for the Italian fashion designer Nolita, which features an anorexic model. The image triggered passionate debate, and was eventually banned in Italy and removed from public places.

Toscani and Benetton must be credited with unleashing fundamental discussions concerning the meaning, purpose, and potentialities of advertising. Yet remaining is an unease for anyone familiar with commercial clients and knowing little more about the Benetton philosophy. Is more really at stake than the need to generate attention? Addressees can exploit this question to relieve themselves of responsibility once again. A social agency, on the other hand, enjoys a different level of credibility–although development organizations rarely expose themselves publicly through such exceptional and realistic images.

CAMEROON AT EYE LEVEL

Michael von Graffenried's large-format photographs of Cameroon, which are printed and displayed on public poster walls, illustrate in an exemplary way the role played by the client in public reception. While Toscani counts in the final analysis as a streetwise public relations strategist who brought his eminently ethical intentions to bear in his work for a financially potent fashion concern, Graffenried intervenes in urban space as a committed artist and photographer. He need not compromise: no profit must be ensured, no quota of donations secured, no scandal provoked. His most recent cycle, *eye on africa*,[3] was produced in collaboration with Fairmed for the organization's fiftieth-anniversary jubilee, but consciously avoided serving as a poster campaign for the organization. In March of 2009, the panoramic images were hung in formats of 125 x 270 cm on public advertising surfaces in five Swiss cities, and simultaneously displayed as a series in front of the Zentrum Paul Klee in Bern.

If Toscani's choice of images was essentially designed to arouse or provoke, then Graffenried's point of view –and hence his intentions as well–is more muted and less spectacular. The dramatism through which Toscani's images call attention to human and ecological catastrophes (just think of his Christomorphic portrait

112 **Atelier Gerhard Blättler / Michael von Graffenried**
2009 CH
[Kamerun – Cameroon, 2008]

of an AIDS sufferer surrounded by his family) is absent from Graffenried's work. The reception of his panoramic photographs featuring people from various social classes engaged in everyday activities does not involve responses of shock or dismay—even ephemeral ones. The perspective is chosen so that it absorbs passers-by into the represented scene. On the occasion of a 2003 exhibition which juxtaposed photographs of Switzerland and Algeria by Graffenried, Harald Szeemann wrote: "Both worlds present themselves to viewers at eye level, hence becoming objective image worlds that are not dramatized by diverse focal points, and which thereby attempt to integrate (art) viewers directly into the depicted events."[4]

With Graffenried, we encounter individuals who invite us to engage in dialogue. And this dialogue occurs on a coequal basis, one that avoids hastily confirming clichéd roles of privilege and underprivileged, familiar and exotic. This relation of equality in the process of perceiving another culture, one that consistently testifies to a respectful attitude on the part of the photographer, is made explicit to the beholder. Perception, then, is conditioned by curiosity and openness in relation to the Other rather than pity and arrogance.

Both Toscani and Graffenried—each in his own way, albeit in wholly different contexts—exploit public space in order to oppose the tastelessness of advertising with an alternative perspective. In so doing, each takes his public seriously, challenging it, inviting it to see differently. They act as contemporary "iconoclasts" who raise vital questions, opposing the one-dimensional world conveyed by consumer advertising, and inciting viewers to new levels of involvement.

Bettina Richter

1 Susan Sontag, *Regarding the Pain of Others* (New York 2001), p 117.
2 Oliviero Toscani, *Die Werbung ist ein lächelndes Aas* (Mannheim 1996), p. 56.
3 Michael von Graffenried, *Michael von Graffenried: eye on africa. Fotografien aus Kamerun / Photographies du Cameroun / Photographs from Cameroon* (Basel 2009).
4 Harald Szeemann, introduction, *Zwischen Welten = Entre deux mondes: Michael von Graffenried*, exh. cat. Kunstmuseum Bern (Bern 2003).

"In my advertisements, I want to communicate with the public about the power of clichés and about platitudes (in the end, advertising is filled with these). About conformity and about the freedom of the spirit. About tolerance. Why do most people simply remain with their initial reactions, with racist or anti-racist tabooization? Why should advertising not function—like art and the media—as a sphere of action for philosophy, an emotional catalyst, a forum for contestation and polemics? Undoubtedly, I was the one who was most surprised by the violent reactions and by the power of racist clichés. At that point, however, I realized that this play with stereotypes offered tremendous possibilities for ridding ourselves of instilled and accepted opinions."
Oliviero Toscani, 1995

Quoted from: Oliviero Toscani, *La Pub est une charogne qui nous sourit* (Paris 1995).

"With my photographs, it is always a question of introducing people who would never encounter one another under normal circumstances. In order to facilitate such encounters, I seek out individuals in order to depict them in authentic situations. Then I insert these images into new surroundings where viewers are confronted by these individuals. That is also why these pictures are shown in such large formats [i.e., as posters—the eds.]. The viewer is drawn into the image, where he finds himself together with the people shown in them. In 'eye on africa,' it was a question of generating such encounters. Swiss viewers engaged with the Africans shown in the panoramas, perhaps reducing the sense of strangeness somewhat. 'eye on africa' shows the multifaceted beauty of African in a way that contrasts with the violence and poverty we have long associated with that continent. Clearly emphasizing this positive trend is the fact that in 2009, an African-American assumed the office of the presidency in the United States of America."
Michael von Graffenried, 2009

Quoted from: www.fairmed.ch/50/dl/ mvg_interview_lang_d.pdf.

In jedem Urlaub werden
Millionen Deutsche
zu Ausländern

114 **Klaus Staeck**
In jedem Urlaub werden Millionen Deutsche
zu Ausländern
1987 DE

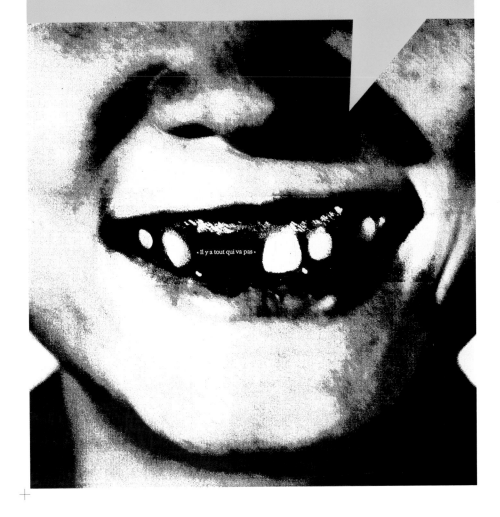

115 **Gérard Paris-Clavel**
– Pas d'achat, pas de bonheur
2002 FR

116 Wirz Werbung AG
Woher haben die Kosovo-Albaner ihre Autoradios? /
Stiftung gegen Rassimus und Antisemitismus, 2003 CH

117 Grendene, Ogilvy & Mather AG
Damit ermöglichen Sie zwei Kindern in Bangladesch die
Schutzimpfung. / Caritas, 2000 CH

118 Wirz Werbung AG
Was machen Thailänderinnen, wenn es dunkel wird? /
Stiftung gegen Rassimus und Antisemitismus, 2003 CH

119 Grendene, Ogilvy & Mather AG
Damit versorgen sie ein Kind in Haiti einen Monat lang
mit einer warmen Mahlzeit. / Caritas, 2000 CH

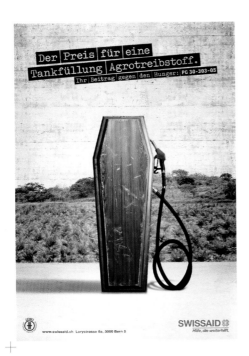

120 Lesch & Frei Werbeagentur AG
Fai come Guglielmo Tell. Centra la libertà. / Swissaid
2003 CH

121 Lesch & Frei Werbeagentur AG
Der Preis für eine Tankfüllung Agrotreibstoff. / Swissaid
2009 CH

122 Bosch & Butz Werbeagentur AG
Machen Sie der Dritten Welt ein Geschenk. / Swissaid
1998 CH

123 Bosch & Butz Werbeagentur
Jetzt können Sie etwas zurückgeben. / Swissaid
1992 CH

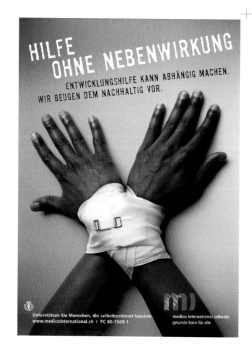

124 Naoki Hirai
Peace / Kyushu Graphic Designers Club, 2000 JP

125 Georgi Eremenko / Aino-Maija Metsola
Artikla 9 – Ihmisoikeuksien Yleismaailmallinen Julistus
60 Vuotta / Amnesty International, 2008 FI

126 Komunikat
Hilfe ohne Nebenwirkung / Medico International
Schweiz, 2008 CH

127 Heidi Franceschini
Danke. / Helvetas, ca. 1991 CH

128 **Grapus**
Nord – Sud
1991 FR

129 **Hochschule für Gestaltung und Kunst Basel**
Secours Suisse d'hiver 95 / Winterhilfe
1995 CH

130 **Impuls Werbung AG / TBWA GGK**
Wegschauen. / Caritas
1999 CH

131 **Ecole d'Art de La Chaux-de-Fonds**
www.soccorso-d-inverno.ch / Winterhilfe
2005 CH

132 **Sophie Rogg**
www.winterhilfe.ch / Winterhilfe
2007 CH

133 **Hochschule für Gestaltung und Kunst Luzern**
Armut geht unter die Haut / Winterhilfe
2009 CH

DIE FREIHEIT NEHM ICH DIR

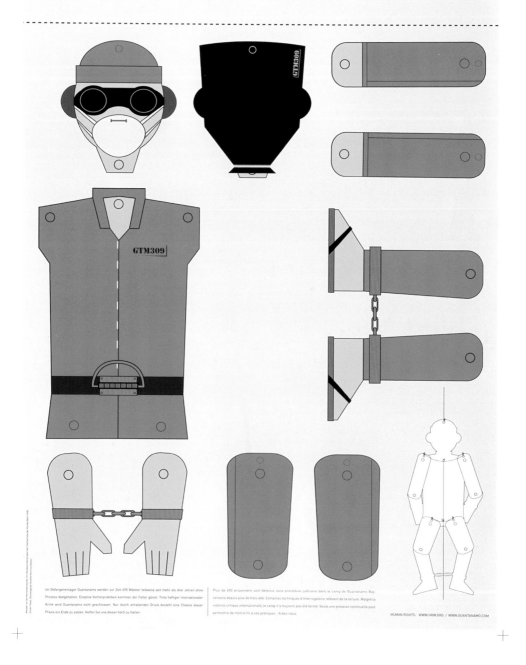

134 **Dimitri Reist**
Die Freiheit nehm ich Dir / Hochschule der Künste Bern
2006 CH

135 **Pierre Neumann**
Wohin würden Sie fliehen? /
Schweizerische Flüchtlingshilfe
1992 CH

136 **Marty Petersen**
All I want is world peace and.../
Visual Concepts International
1989 US

PEACE IN THE CAGE

平和が隠れている

世界の軍事支出： 1分間で100万ドル	World armaments expenditure : A million dollars a minute	Мировые расходы на вооружение: 1 000 000 долларов в минуту
Rüstungsausgaben der Welt: **1 Million $ pro Minute**	Dépenses mondiales d'armement : 1 000 000 dollars/minute	世 界 軍 備 費 用： 每 分 鐘 百 万 美 元
O mundo gasta com armamentos 1.000.000 de dólares por minuto	Gastos mundiales en armamentos : 1 000 000 de dólares por minuto	الإنفاق العالمي على السلاح ١٠٠٠٠٠٠ دولار في الدقيقة

137 **Masuteru Aoba**
Peace in the cage
1982 JP

138 **Masuteru Aoba**
The real weight of peace
1982 JP

139 **Masuteru Aoba**
Energy is for *peace*
1982 JP

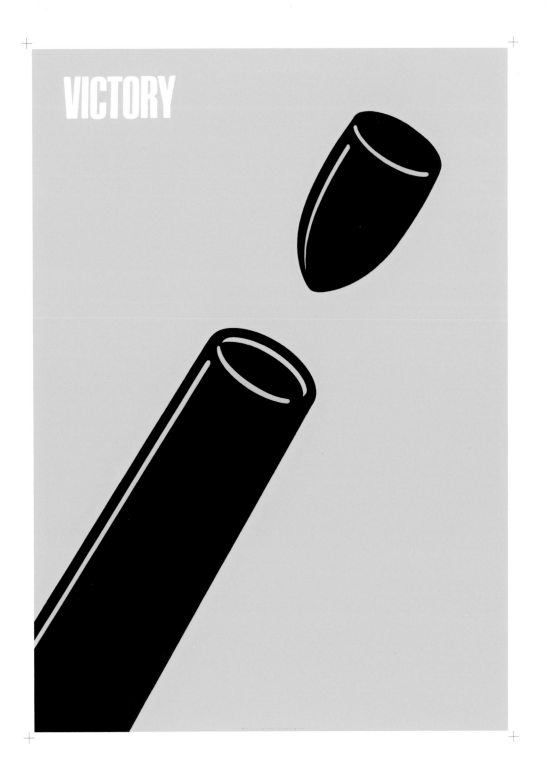

140 **Shigeo Fukuda**
Victory / International Poster Biennial Warsaw
1975 JP

141 **Gérard Paris-Clavel**
– Qui a peur d'une femme?
1997 FR

Katalog

Alle abgebildeten Plakate stammen aus der Plakatsammlung des Museum für Gestaltung Zürich. Das Copyright liegt bei den Autoren.
103–113 © Michael von Graffenried, www.mvgphoto.com
© 2009 ProLitteris, Zürich: Klaus Staeck 12, 25, 114; Niklaus Troxler 52.

Die Daten des Katalogs folgen den Rubriken Gestaltung, Auftraggeber, Plakattext, Erscheinungsjahr, Erscheinungsland, Drucktechnik und Format. Dabei gelten insbesondere folgende Regelungen:

Auftraggeber: Dem Thema entsprechend ist es besonders aufschlussreich, die für die Botschaft des Plakats verantwortlichen Auftraggeber zu kennen. Die Auftraggeber werden jedoch nur angegeben, wo sie mit Sicherheit zu eruieren waren. Mehrere Auftraggeber sind mit dem Zeichen / voneinander abgetrennt.

Plakattext: Die beste Textwiedergabe bildet die Abbildung des Plakates selbst. Darum wird hier eine vereinfachte Form wiedergegeben, welche nur die aussagekräftigen Textbestandteile berücksichtigt. Allfällige Umstellungen dienen der Verständlichkeit. Das Zeichen / oder – trennt inhaltliche Texteinheiten.

Erscheinungsland: Das Erscheinungsland wird mit dem international gebräuchlichen ISO-Code angegeben.

Format: Die Angaben werden in der Abfolge Höhe × Breite und in cm gemacht. Weil die Plakate oft nicht exakt rechtwinklig geschnitten sind, werden die Abmessungen auf halbe cm aufgerundet.

Die Plakatgeschichte ist ein junges Forschungsgebiet – verlässliche Hinweise sind rar. Jeder Hinweis und jede Ergänzung sind willkommen:
plakatsammlung@museum-gestatung.ch

Catalogue

All posters reproduced are from the Museum für Gestaltung Zürich's Poster Collection. The copyrights are held by the authors.
103–113 © Michael von Graffenried, www.mvgphoto.com
© 2009 ProLitteris, Zürich: Klaus Staeck 12, 25, 114; Niklaus Troxler 52.

The data listed in the catalogue is broken down into the following sections: designer, client, poster title and/or text, year and country of first appearance, printing technique, and size. In particular, the following rules have been applied:

Client: Depending upon the theme, of special relevance is the identity of the client responsible for the poster's message. Clients are identified, however, only when their identity could be ascertained with certainty. Multiple clients are separated from one another by a slash.

Poster text: The poster itself provides the best version of the text, and thus a simplified form is used which provides only the most meaningful elements. Any rearrangements that have been made are for purposes of intelligibility. A slash mark or en-dash separates textual units by content.

Country of first appearance: The country of first appearance is identified by the internationally accepted ISO code.

Format: The dimensions are given in centimeters as height × width. Because posters are often not cut exactly at right angles, the dimensions are rounded off to the half-centimeter.

The history of posters is a recent field of research– reliable information is rare. Any further references or additional material are welcome:
plakatsammlung@museum-gestaltung.ch

1 Pierre Mendell (1929–2008)
Pierre Mendell
Vor Gott sind alle Menschen
gleich – All are equal before God
1995 DE Offset 119 × 84 cm

2 Oliviero Toscani (1942–)
Benetton Group S.p.A.
United Colors of Benetton.
1992 IT Offset 175 × 118 cm

3 Suunnittelutoimisto Both
Timo Berry (1973–)
Amnesty International – Finland
Amnesty International / Plakatgestalter für Amnesty: Recht auf freie Mei-
nungsäusserung – Amnesty International / Posterdesigners for Amnesty:
Freedom of Expression
2003 FI Offset 100 × 70 cm

4 Grapus
Artis
Reich / Arm – Rich / Poor
1989 FR Siebdruck – Screenprint
84 × 59,5 cm

5 Naoki Hirai (1960–)
Naoki Hirai
Ist dein Baby sicher? Schütze dein
Kind for verseuchtem Wasser.
Is your baby safe? Save your child
from the polluted water.
2001 JP Offset 103 × 73 cm

6 Lex Drewinski (1951–)
Friedensinitiative Berlin
Rassismus – Racism
1993 DE Siebdruck – Screenprint
70 × 100 cm

7 Mitsuo Katsui (1931–)
Japan Graphic Designers Association Inc. (JAGDA)
AIR / I'm here. The JAGDA Peace
and Environment Poster Exhibition
1993 JP Offset 103 × 73 cm

8 Norman Clayton
Environmental Protection Agency
(EPA)
global denken / lokal handeln /
1990 / Earth day – think globally /
act locally / 1990 / Earth day
1990 US Offset 66,5 × 44 cm

9 Lanny Sommese (1943–)
Lanny Sommese
1986 / International Year of Peace
1986 US Siebdruck /
Irisdruck – Screenprint /
Iris print 85,5 × 60,5 cm

10 Hirokatsu Hijikata
Niemand will eine getarnte Erde!!
No one wants a camouflaged earth!!
ca. 1990 JP Siebdruck – Screenprint 103 × 72,5 cm

11 Anonym
C.P.R. Environmental Education
Centre Madras
Es gibt nur eine Erde … Schütze sie
There is only one earth … Save it
ca. 1996 IN Offset 76 × 50,5 cm

12 Klaus Staeck (1983–)
Klaus Staeck
Die Mietsache ist schonend zu
behandeln und in gutem Zustand
zurückzugeben
The rentals should be well treated
and returned in good condition
1983 DE Offset 84 × 59,5 cm

13 Gérard Paris-Clavel (1943–)
Gérard Paris-Clavel, in Zusammenarbeit mit – in collaboration with
Service d'action culturel de la ville
de Blanc-Mesnil
Money World
1992 FR Siebdruck – Screenprint
160 × 120 cm

14 Spillmann, Felser, Leo Burnett AG
Brot für Alle / Fastenopfer
Eigentlich sieht die Welt so aus.
The world really looks like that.
2009 CH Offset 42 × 30 cm

15 Spinas Gemperle GmbH
Caritas
Hngr. Alle 5 Sekunden reisst der
Hunger ein Kind aus dem Leben.
Hngr. Every five seconds, hunger
claims the life of a child.
2008 CH Offset 170 × 117 cm

16 Hoffmann, York & Compton
Hunger Task Force
Es gibt Schlimmeres im Leben als
hungrig schlafenzugehen. Eines ist
hungrig aufzuwachen.
There are worse things in life than
going to bed hungry. One of them
is waking up hungry.
1991 US Siebdruck – Screenprint
60 × 46 cm

17 Peter Cohen (1955–)
Coalition for the Homeless
"Iss auf. Es gibt es tausende
von hungernden Menschen
in New York City."
"Finish your food. There are
thousands of starving people
in New York City."
1990 US Offset 62,5 × 45 cm

18 Ina Hattenhauer (1982–)
Stiftung Nord-Süd-Brücken
Menschen in Entwicklungsländern
brauchen Massnahmen, die nicht
nur heute helfen, sondern auch
übermorgen wirken.
People in developing countries
need assistance, not just for today,
but for the day after tomorrow.
2005 DE Digitaldruck – Digital print
84 × 60 cm

19 Publicis Werbeagentur AG
Terre des hommes
Wenn Kinder sich nicht wehren
können. Help – When children
cannot defend themselves. Help
2006 CH Offset 170 × 116 cm

20 Masuteru Aoba (1939–)
Photo: Hiroshi Koiwai
Das Brot ist für den *Frieden*
The bread is for *peace*
1984 JP Offset 103 × 73 cm

21 Pierre Mendell Design Studio
Annette Kröger (1964–)
Pierre Mendell (1929–2008)
Pierre Mendell Design Studio
teile – share
2004 DE Offset 118,5 × 84 cm

22 Pentagram Design New York
Woody Pirtle (1944–)
Amnesty International USA
Artikel 25 / Der Allgemeinen
Erklärung der Menschenrechte /
Jeder hat das Recht auf einen
angemessenen Lebensstandard
Article 25 / From the Universal
Declaration of Human Rights /
Everyone Has the Right to an
Adequate Standard of Living
2002 US Offset 60,5 × 45,5 cm

23 Teemu Mäki (1967–)
Amnesty International – Finland
Artikla 29 / Ihmisoikeuksien
Yleismaailmallinen Julistus
60 Vuotta
Artikel 29 / 60 Jahre Allgemeine
Erklärung der Menschenrechte
Article 29 / Universal Declaration of
Human Rights: 60 Years
2008 FI Offset 100 × 70 cm

24 Cyan
Detlef Fiedler (1955–)
Daniela Haufe (1966–)
ohne Text – no text
[Mit diesem Plakat wurden Chiquita-
Werbeplakate überklebt, die in
Berlin während einer Hungersnot
in Afrika verbreitet wurden.]
[Copies of this poster were pasted
over Chiquita ads in Berlin during a
famine in Africa.]
1994 DE Offset 84 × 119 cm

25 Klaus Staeck (1938–)
Klaus Staeck
Das Neue PAL / Schlachtfrisch aus
der Dose. – The new PAL / Fresh
meat from a can.
1977 DE Offset DE 83,5 × 59 cm

26 Luba Lukova (1960–)
International Anti-Poverty Law
Center
Krieg Verbrechen – War Crime
1999 US Siebdruck – Screenprint
88,5 × 63 cm

27 Tiitu Takalo (1967–)
Amnesty International – Finland
Artikla 25 / Ihmisoikeuksien Yleis-
maailmallinen Julistus 60 Vuotta
Artikel 25 / 60 Jahre Allgemeine
Erklärung der Menschenrechte
Article 25 / Universal Declaration
of Human Rights: 60 Years
2008 FI Offset 100 × 70 cm

28 Luba Lukova (1960–)
International Anti-Poverty Law
Center
Hunger Verbrechen – Hunger Crime
1999 US Siebdruck – Screenprint
88,5 × 63 cm

29 Luba Lukova (1960–)
International Anti-Poverty Law
Center
Sudan
1999 US Siebdruck – Screenprint
100 × 69,5 cm

30 U. G. Sato (1935–)
Save the Children Organization
Rette hungernde Kinder
Save hungry children
1998 JP Siebdruck – Screenprint
175 × 118 cm

31 Publicis Werbeagentur AG
Médecins sans Frontières
Schnelle medizinische Hilfe.
Rapid medical assistance.
2006 CH Offset 125 × 268 cm

32 Anonym
Humanist Association of Hong Kong
Öffentlich zu rauchen löst heftigere
Reaktionen aus als solche Ge-
schichten. Wo bleibt unser Mass?
Nichtraucher für Raucherrechte
Smoking in public receives a more
violent reaction nowadays than
stories like this. Where has our perspective gone? Non-Smokers for
the Rights of Smokers
1996 HK Siebdruck – Screenprint
50,5 × 77 cm

33 Anonym
Humanist Association of Hongkong
Im Büro eine Zigarette anzuzünden,
kann Sie eine Anklage wegen Bron-
chialproblemen kosten. Wohin führt
das? Konzentrieren wir uns auf das,
was zählt. Nichtraucher für Raucherrechte
Light a cigarette in the office and
someone's bound to take you to
court as the cause of their bronchial
problems. Where does it end?
Because we'd like to begin focusing
on the matters that matter. Non-
Smokers for the Rights of Smokers
1996 HK Siebdruck – Screenprint
50,5 × 77 cm

34 Gaudenz Tscharner AG
Fred Bauer (1928–)
Helvetas
L'acqua fonte di vita / Helvetas aiuta
i paesi del Terzo Mondo. E voi?
Wasser / Lebensquelle / Helvetas
hilft den Ländern der Dritten Welt.
Und Ihr? – Water / Source of life /
Helvetas helps the countries of the
Third World. And you?
1986 CH Offset 128 × 90,5 cm

35 Anonym
Internationales Komitee vom Rotem
Kreuz (IKRK) – International
Committee of the Red Cross (ICRC)
Wir unterrichten / Vermitteln die Mittel
zum Schutz der Menschenwürde
We teach / Providing the means
to safeguard human dignity
ca. 2005 CH Offset 84 × 59,5 cm

36 Spinas Gemperle GmbH
Helvetas
Für 1,1 Milliarden Menschen kein
Witz. Unverseuchtes Trinkwasser
verhindert tödliche Krankheiten.
For 1.1 billion people, it's no joke.
Uncontaminated drinking water
prevents deadly disease.
2008 CH Offset 170 × 116,5 cm

37 Anonym
Internationales Komitee vom Roten
Kreuz (IKRK) – International Com-
mittee of the Red Cross (ICRC)
Wir löschen Durst / Versorgen
Konfliktopfer mit frischem Wasser
We quench thirst / Providing conflict
victims with fresh water
ca. 2005 CH Offset 84 × 59,5 cm

38 Scherer Kleiber Creative
Direction AG
United Nations International Children's
Emergency Fund (UNICEF) Schweiz
Mutter spielen, weil man keine hat.
Being a mother to those who have
none.
1988 CH Offset 128 × 271 cm

39 Publicis Werbeagentur AG
Migros-Genossenschafts-Bund
(MGB)
Was wir unter Kinderarbeit verste-
hen. – What we mean by child labor.
2006 CH Offset 128 × 271 cm

40 Homberger & Minet Graphic
Design
Terre des hommes
«Ich fragte, weshalb ich nicht zur
Schule dürfte. Es hiess, ich solle
arbeiten. Ich arbeite immer bis spät
in die Nacht.» Acácias, ein Haus-
mädchen in Brasilien / Kinder werden weltweit als Hausangestellte
ausgebeutet. Wir setzen uns für sie
ein. – "I asked why I couldn't go
to school. I was told I had to work.
I worked until late into the night."
Acácias, a Brazilian housemaid /
Children worldwide are exploited
as domestic servants. We are
helping them.
2004 CH Offset 128 × 271 cm

41 Publicis Werbeagentur AG
Photo: Rocco Rorandelli (1973–)
Terre des hommes
Es gibt einen Weg aus jedem
Unrecht. Wir kämpfen gegen Kinder-
arbeit.
There is a solution to every injustice.
We are fighting against child labor.
2007 CH Offset 128 × 271 cm

42 Spinas Gemperle GmbH
Terre des hommes
Dank Ihnen leben Jugendliche in
Brasilien vom Mais. Statt vom Müll.
Thanks to you, children in Brazil
live from corn. Not from trash.
2007 CH Siebdruck – Screenprint
128 × 271 cm

43 Spinas Gemperle GmbH
Photo: Simon B. Opladen (1976–)
Fairmed
Stoppen wir Lepra. Heute /
in 2 Jahren / in 5 Jahren – Putting
an end to leprosy. Today /
In 2 years / In 5 years
2009 CH Offset 128 × 271 cm

44 Hans Erni (1909–)
Aktion "Rettet den Wald"
rettet den Wald – save our woods
1983 CH Offset 128 × 90,5 cm

45 Andreas Karl (1958–)
Bund für Umwelt und Naturschutz
Deutschland
Der tropische Regenwald
The tropical rain forest
1995 DE Offset 83,5 × 59 cm

46 Sébastien Courtois (1973–)
Sébastien Courtois
Stoppt die Abholzung
Stop deforestation
2005 FR Siebdruck – Screenprint
102 × 70 cm

47 Anonym
Direction de la Coopération au développement et de l'aide humanitaire
Chaque mois disparaît dans le
monde l'équivalent de la forêt
suisse … – Jeden Monat verschwin-
det auf der Welt das Äquivalent des
Schweizer Waldes… – Every month
the equivalent of the Swiss forests
disappears from the world…
1983 CH Siebdruck – Screenprint
70 × 50 cm

48 U. G. Sato (1935–)
Japan Graphic Designers Association Inc. (JAGDA)
I'm here. The JAGDA Peace and
Environment Poster Exhibition
1993 JP Siebdruck – Screenprint
103 × 70 cm

49 Select International
World Wildlife Fund (WWF)
Deutschland
3 Euro retten seine Welt. Retten
Sie mit: wwf.de – 3 euros rescues
his world. Help at: wwf.de
2008 DE Offset 59,5 × 42 cm

50 Savaş Çekiç (1960–)
Stil Matbaasi
ohne Text – no text
1998 TR Offset 69 × 48 cm

51 U. G. Sato (1935–)
U. G. Sato
Wohin kann die Natur gehen ?
Where can Nature go?
1993 JP Siebdruck – Screenprint
102,7 × 72,6 cm

52 Niklaus Troxler (1947–)
Niklaus Troxler
ohne Text – no text
1992 CH Siebdruck – Screenprint
128 × 90,5 cm

53 Savaş Çekiç (1960–)
Stil Matbaasi
ohne Text – no text
1998 TR Offset 69 × 48 cm

54 Masuteru Aoba (1939–)
Japan Graphic Designers
Association Inc. (JAGDA)
Leaves, like the things of man,
you / With your fresh thoughts care
for, can you?
1992 JP Offset 103 × 73 cm

55 Sergej Kužavskij (1966–)
Photo: A. Koval'
World Wildlife Fund (WWF)
Spasti choču zemnuju krasotu … /
A.S. Puškin – Retten will ich der
Erde Pracht … / A.S. Puskin
I want to rescue the earth's splen-
dors … / A.S. Pushkin
ca. 1995 RU Offset 60 × 90 cm

56 Tomoko Inue
Masato Watanabe
Japan Graphic Designers
Association Inc. (JAGDA)
I'm here. The JAGDA Peace and
Environment Poster Exhibition
ca. 1993 JP Offset 103 × 73 cm

57 Oliviero Toscani (1942–)
Photo: Steve McCurry (1950–)
Benetton Group S.p.A.
United Colors of Benetton.
1992 IT Offset 30 × 42 cm

58 Publicis Werbeagentur AG
Migros-Genossenschafts-Bund
(MGB)
Warum auch Fische Ferien brau-
chen. – Why fish need holidays too.
2006 CH Offset 128 × 271 cm

59 Hochschule für Gestaltung
und Kunst Luzern (HGK Luzern)
Pierre de Senarclens (1968–)
Photo: René Rittler
Stadt Luzern Umweltschutz (UWS
Luzern)
Beach Party / Klimaveränderung –
wann werden wir aus Schaden klug?
Beach Party / Climate change –
When will we get it?
1995 CH Siebdruck – Screenprint
128 × 271 cm

60 Hochschule für Gestaltung
und Kunst Luzern (HGK Luzern)
Pierre de Senarclens (1968–)
Photo: René Rittler
Stadt Luzern Umweltschutz (UWS
Luzern)
Kreuzfahrt / Verändern Sie sich,
damit sich das Klima nicht verändert. – Cruise / Change yourself
so that the climate doesn't need to.
1995 CH Siebdruck – Screenprint
128 × 271 cm

61 Hochschule für Gestaltung
und Kunst Luzern (HGK Luzern)
Pierre de Senarclens (1968–)
Photo: René Rittler
Stadt Luzern Umweltschutz
(UWS Luzern)
Whirl Pool / Stopp der Klimaver-
änderung!
Whirlpool / Stop climate change!
1995 CH Siebdruck – Screenprint
128 × 271 cm

62 Kiyotaka Hotta (1951–)
Japan Graphic Designers
Association Inc. (JAGDA)
Wa Wa Water
1991 JP Offset 103 × 73 cm

63 Surič Design
Jurij Surkov (1961–)
L'association pour une banque
d'images: L'eau pour l'humanité
Wasser für die Menschheit.
Water for human kind.
2000 RU Siebdruck – Screenprint
99 × 69 cm

64 Takahiro Shima (1938–)
Japan Graphic Designers
Association Inc. (JAGDA)
Wasser ist Leben
Water is life
1990 JP Offset 103 × 73 cm

65 James Victore (1962–)
Earth Day
ohne Text – no text
1995 US Siebdruck – Screenprint
99,5 × 68,5 cm

66 Naoki Hirai (1960–)
Naoki Hirai
Schützt das Wasser
Save The Water
2002 JP Offset 103 × 73 cm

67 Gerda Frisch
Amnesty International Deutschland
AI hilft gewaltlosen politischen
Gefangenen in aller Welt / AI setzt
sich ein gegen Folter und Todesstrafe / AI existiert auch in ihrer Stadt
AI helps defenseless political
prisoners around the world / AI fights
torture and the death penalty /
AI can be found in your town.
ca. 1985 DE Siebdruck – Screenprint 84 × 59,5 cm

68 Ralph Schraivogel (1960–)
Allianz Deutscher Designer e.V.
(AGD) / Bund Deutscher Grafik-
Designer e.V. (BDG) / Verband der
Grafik Designer e.V. (VDGD) / Verein
für Kommunalwissenschaften
«Deutschland über Alles»
"Germany above all"
1993 CH Siebdruck – Screenprint
84,5 × 59,4 cm

69 Germar Wambach (1962–)
German Wambach
Terror / Error / Was keiner geglaubt
haben wird / Was keiner gewusst
haben konnte
Terror / Error / What no one would
have believed / What no one could
have known
1992 DE Siebdruck – Screenprint
80 × 60 cm

70 Claude Baillargeon (1949–)
Mairie de Bagnolet
SOS Injustices
1990 FR Siebdruck – Screenprint
120 × 80 cm

71 Ralph Schraivogel (1960–)
Sacha Wigdorovits
Live – Evil
2009 CH Siebdruck – Screenprint
128 × 90,5 cm

72 anschlaege.de
Janneke De Rooij (1985–)
Christian Lagé (1976–)
Axel Watzke (1975–)
Kampnagel, Internationale Kultur-
fabrik GmbH
«Mal ganz ehrlich, können Sie mit
100 Euro im Monat auskommen?»
Hier spricht Barmbek! Barmbek.TV
"Honestly, could you survive on
100 € per month?" Barmbek speaks
here! Barmbek.TV
2007 DE Siebdruck – Screenprint
86 × 61 cm

73 Oliviero Toscani (1942–)
Photo: Oliviero Toscani
Benetton Group S.p.A.
United Colors of Benetton. Zum
Tode verurteilt / David Leroy Skaggs
Condemned to death / David Leroy
Skaggs
2000 IT Offset 170 × 117 cm

74 anschlaege.de
Janneke De Rooij (1985–)
Christian Lagé (1976–)
Axel Watzke (1975–)
Kampnagel, Internationale Kultur-
fabrik GmbH
«Jeder wird ernten, was er sät. Wird
er Liebe säen, wird er auch Liebe
ernten.» Hier spricht Barmbek!
Barmbek.TV
"Each will reap what he has sown.
If he has reaped love, he will
sow love." Barmbek speaks here!
Barmbek.TV
2007 DE Siebdruck –
Screenprint 86 × 61 cm

75 Oliviero Toscani (1942–)
Photo: Oliviero Toscani
Benetton Group S.p.A.
United Colors of Benetton. Zum
Tode verurteilt / Leroy Orange
Condemned to death / Leroy Orange
2000 IT Offset 170 × 117 cm

76 Gunter Rambow (1938–)
Deutscher Gewerkschaftsbund
(DGB) / Interkultureller Rat in
Deutschland e.V.
Deutschland den Deutschen / Ham-
burg den Hamburgern / Pinneberg
den Pinnebergern / Rassismus
macht einsam
Germany for the Germans /
Hamburg for the Hamburgers /
Pinneberg for the Pinnebergers /
Racism makes us lonely.
1995 DE Offset 118,5 × 84 cm

77 Andreas Fechner (1963–)
Bernward Kraft Verein für
Kommunalwissenschaften
Anita S. – Mensch.
Anita S. – Human being.
ca. 1992 DE Offset 83,5 × 59 cm

78 Gunter Rambow (1938–)
Deutscher Gewerkschaftsbund
(DGB) / Interkultureller Rat in
Deutschland e.V.
Deutschland den Deutschen /
Frankfurt for the Frankfurters /
Seckbach for the Seckbachers /
Herr Meier for Herr Meier / Rassis-
mus macht einsam – Germany
for the Germans / Frankfurt for the
Frankfurters / Seckbach for the
Seckbachers / Herr Meier for Herr
Meier / Racism makes us lonely.
1995 DE Offset 118,5 × 84 cm

79 Andreas Fechner (1963–)
Bernward Kraft
Verein für Kommunalwissenschaften
Tom D. – Mensch.
Tom D. – Human being.
ca. 1992 DE Offset 83,5 × 59 cm

80 Roland Piltz (1978–)
Aisha Ronniger (1982–)
Kunsthochschule Berlin Weissensee
Scientologist / Gonçalo /
Addicted / Batanda
2007 DE Siebdruck –
Screenprint / Montage 86 × 65 cm

81 Roland Piltz (1978–)
Aisha Ronniger (1982–)
Kunsthochschule Berlin Weissensee
Sikh / Bulle / Schmidt
Sikh / Cop / Schmidt
2007 DE Siebdruck –
Screenprint / Montage 86 × 65 cm

82 Roland Piltz (1978–)
Aisha Ronniger (1982–)
Kunsthochschule Berlin Weissensee
Istanbul / Hero / Parvati / Sarajevo
2007 DE Siebdruck –
Screenprint / Montage 86 × 65 cm

83 Roland Piltz (1978–)
Aisha Ronniger (1982–)
Kunsthochschule Berlin Weissensee
New York / Vladimir / Arbeitslos
New York / Vladimir / Unemployed
2007 DE Siebdruck –
Screenprint / Montage 86 × 65 cm

84 Urs Grünig (1947–)
Amnesty International Schweiz
Menschenrechte für Alle / Werden
Sie mit Amnesty International
aktiv! – Human rights for all /
Join Amnesty International!
1999 CH Siebdruck – Screenprint
128 × 89,5 cm

85 James Victore (1962–)
Legal Defense and Educational
Fund (LDF) / American Civil Liberties
Union (ACLU)
Rassismus und Todesstrafe /
Doppelbestrafung / _ _ g g _ r
Racism and the Death Penalty /
Double Justice / _ _ g g _ r
1993 US Offset 82,5 × 58,5 cm

86 James Victore (1962–)
James Victore
Rassismus – Racism
1993 US Siebdruck – Screenprint
66,5 × 102 cm

87 James Victore (1962–)
Anti-Defamation League of
New York (ADL)
Hass – Hate
1997 US Siebdruck – Screenprint
127,5 × 86,5 cm

88 James Victore (1962–)
Legal Defense and Educational
Fund (LDF)
Die Todesstrafe spottet der
Gerechtigkeit
The Death Penalty Mocks Justice
1995 US Offset 97 × 66 cm

89 Eva Kemény
László Sós
Ministry of Environment and
Water Supply
ohne Text – no text
1988 HU Siebdruck – Screenprint
98 × 68 cm

90 Eva Kemény
László Sós
Ministry of Environment and
Water Supply
ohne Text – no text
1988 HU Siebdruck – Screenprint
98 × 68 cm

91 Jerry Torchia
Amnesty International USA
Die meisten Staaten hätten diese
Kinder in die Förderschule
geschickt. Virginia schickt sie in
den Tod. – Most states would have
put these kids in reform school.
Virginia put them to death.
1992 US Offset 51 × 61 cm

92 Jerry Torchia
Amnesty International USA
Vielleicht hätte man die Todesstrafe
schon vor langer Zeit abschaffen
sollen. – Maybe the death penalty
should have been eliminated a
long time ago.
1992 US Offset 51 × 61 cm

93 Stephan Bundi (1950–)
Amnesty International Schweiz
Stoppt die Folter. – Stop torture.
1985 CH Siebdruck – Screenprint
128 × 90,5 cm

94 Meta-Cultura
Helvetas
«Die Weissen denken zuviel»/
Ein Dorfchef aus Mali
"White men think too much"/
A village chief from Mali
1993 CH Siebdruck – Screenprint
128 × 90,5 cm

95 Vladimir Antonov
Amnesty International Norwegen –
Norway
Amnesty International
1993 NO Lithografie – Lithograph
84 × 59,5 cm

96 Oliviero Toscani (1942–)
Photo: Yves Gellie (1953–)
Benetton Group S.p.A.
United Colors of Benetton.
1992 IT Offset 30 × 42 cm

97 Oliviero Toscani (1942–)
Photo: Oliviero Toscani
Benetton Group S.p.A.
United Colors of Benetton.
1989 IT Offset 30 × 42 cm

98 Oliviero Toscani (1942–)
Photo: Oliviero Toscani
Benetton Group S.p.A.
United Colors of Benetton.
1991 IT Offset 30 × 42 cm

99 Oliviero Toscani (1942–)
Photo: Patrick Robert (1958–)
Benetton Group S.p.A.
United Colors of Benetton.
1992 IT Offset 30 × 42 cm

100 Oliviero Toscani (1942–)
Photo: Therese Frare (1958–)
Benetton Group S.p.A.
United Colors of Benetton.
1992 IT Offset 30 × 42 cm

101 Oliviero Toscani (1942–)
Photo: Oliviero Toscani
Benetton Group S.p.A.
United Colors of Benetton.
1991 IT Offset 30 × 42 cm

102 Oliviero Toscani (1942–)
Photo: Oliviero Toscani
Benetton Group S.p.A.
United Colors of Benetton.
Weiss/Schwarz/Gelb
White/Black/Yellow
1996 IT Offset 30 × 42 cm

103–113 Atelier Gerhard Blättler/
Michael von Graffenried (1957–)
Photo: Michael von Graffenried
(Kamerun – Cameroon 2008)
Michael von Graffenried,
in Zusammenarbeit mit –
in collaboration with Fairmed
2009 CH Siebdruck – Screenprint
128 × 271 cm

103 Openair-Musikfestival
«Couleurs Urbaines», Yaoundé,
Kamerun, 19. Juni 2008 – Couleurs
Urbaines, open-air music festival,
Yaoundé, Cameroon, June 19, 2008

104 Grossverteiler von importierter
Gebrauchtkleidung, Markt von
Mboppi, Douala – Distributor
of imported used clothing, market
at Mboppi, Douala

105 Jogger in Bafoussam, West-
Kamerun – Jogger in Bafoussam,
western Cameroon

106 Altkleiderverkäufer in
Bafoussam – Seller of old clothing
in Bafoussam

107 Ankunft der High-Society
Damen zur Einsetzung des Präfekten
von Wouri, Douala – Arrival of high-
society ladies for the appointment of
the prefect of Wouri, Douala

108 Polizeigrenadiere, Douala
Police grenadiers, Douala

109 Vorbereitung für die Einset-
zungszeremonie des Präfekten von
Wouri, Douala – Preparation for
a ceremonial appointment of the
prefect at Wouri, Douala

110 Autounfall auf der Strasse
nach Wum, Nord-West-Kamerun
Car accident on a street past Wum,
northwestern Cameroon

111 Die Verzierung der Kalebasse
auf dem Kopf verrät den Zivilstand
der Kirdi-Frauen. Markt von Tourou, Extremer Norden – Calabash
headdresses reveal the marital sta-
tus of women in Kirdi. Market
of Tourou, extreme north

112 Bei Membza, Mandara-Berge,
Extremer Norden – Near Membza,
Mandara Mountains, extreme north

113 Sonnenuntergang am Atlan-
tischen Ozean in Kribi, der «Riviera
von Kamerun» – Sunset over the
Atlantic Ocean at Kribi, the "Riviera
of Cameroon"

114 Klaus Staeck (1938–)
Klaus Staeck
In jedem Urlaub werden Millionen
Deutsche zu Ausländern
During each vacation season,
millions of Germans become
foreigners.
1987 DE Offset 83 × 59,5 cm

115 Gérard Paris-Clavel (1943–)
Gérard Paris-Clavel
[Teil einer seit 1995 konzipierten
Plakatserie "Il y a tout qui va pas"
in Zusammenarbeit mit dem
Stedelijk Museum und der Stadt
Fontenay sous-Bois]
[Part of the poster series "Il y a
tout qui va pas" conceived begin-
ning in 1995 in collaboration with
the Stedelijk Museum and the
town of Fontenay sous-Bois]
– Pas d'achat, pas de bonheur
– Ohne Shoppen kein Glück
– No shopping, no happiness
2002 FR Siebdruck – Screenprint
175 × 118,5 cm

116 Wirz Werbung AG
Stiftung gegen Rassismus und
Antisemitismus (GRA)
Woher haben die Kosovo-Albaner
ihre Autoradios? Aus dem Fachgeschäft, wie die meisten Schweizer
auch. – Where do Kosovo Albanians
get their car radios? At a store,
like most Swiss people.
2003 CH Gigaplot 128 × 89,5 cm

117 Grendene, Ogilvy & Mather AG
Caritas
Damit ermöglichen Sie zwei Kindern
in Bangladesch die Schutzimpfung.
This will allow the vaccination of two
children in Bangladesh.
2000 CH Offset 170 × 118 cm

118 Wirz Werbung AG
Stiftung gegen Rassimus und
Antisemitismus (GRA)
Was machen Thailänderinnen,
wenn es dunkel wird? Licht, wie
die meisten Schweizerinnen auch.
What do Thai women do when
it gets dark? Turn on the lights,
like most Swiss women.
2003 CH Gigaplot 128 × 89,5 cm

119 Grendene, Ogilvy & Mather AG
Caritas
Damit versorgen sie ein Kind in Haiti
einen Monat lang mit einer warmen
Mahlzeit.
Enough to provide a child in Haiti
with hot meals for a month.
2000 CH Offset 170 × 118 cm

120 Lesch & Frei Werbeagentur AG
Swissaid
Fai come Guglielmo Tell. Centra la
libertà. – Mach es wie Wilhelm Tell.
Es geht um Freiheit. – Do like
William Tell. A question of freedom.
2003 CH Offset 170 × 117 cm

121 Lesch & Frei Werbeagentur AG
Swissaid
Der Preis für eine Tankfüllung
Agrotreibstoff. Ihr Beitrag gegen
den Hunger: PC 30-303-05
The price of a full tank of agrofuel.
Your contribution to combating
hunger: PC 30-303-05
2009 CH Offset 170 × 117 cm

122 Bosch & Butz Werbeagentur
AG
Swissaid
Hilfe, die weiterhilft. Machen Sie
der Dritten Welt ein Geschenk. –
Help toward self-help. Make a gift
to the Third World.
1998 CH Offset 170 × 117 cm

123 Bosch & Butz Werbeagentur AG
Swissaid
500 Jahre lang wurde genommen.
Jetzt können Sie etwas zurück–
geben: Telefon 155 18 80.
The taking went on for 500 years.
Now you can give something back:
Call 155 18 80.
1992 CH Offset 170 × 117 cm

124 Naoki Hirai (1960–)
Kyushu Graphic Designers Club
Friede / Niemand begrüsst Atom-
waffen. – Peace / Nobody welcomes
nuclear weapons.
2000 JP Offset 103 × 73 cm

125 Georgi Eremenko (1981–)
Aino-Maija Metsola (1983–)
Amnesty International – Finland
Artikla 9 / Ihmisoikeuksien Yleis-
maailmallinen Julistus 60 Vuotta
Artikel 9 / 60 Jahre Allgemeine
Erklärung der Menschenrechte
Article 9 / Universal Declaration
of Human Rights: 60 Years
2008 FI Offset 100 × 70 cm

126 Komunikat
Isabelle Blümlein (1970–)
Urs Gägauf (1969–)
Photo: Isabelle Blümlein
Medico International Schweiz
Hilfe ohne Nebenwirkung /
Entwicklungshilfe kann abhängig
machen. Wir beugen dem nachhaltig
vor. – Help without side-effects /
development aid can lead to depen-
dency. We prevent this long-term.
2008 CH Offset 170 × 116,5 cm

127 Heidi Franceschini
Helvetas
Danke. – Thanks.
ca. 1991 CH Offset 128 × 90,5 cm

128 Grapus
Pierre Bernard (1942–)
Gérard Paris-Clavel (1943–)
Grapus
Nord / Sud / Nous travaillons
ensemble – Nord / Süd / Wir arbeiten
zusammen – North / South /
We're working together
1991 FR Siebdruck – Screenprint
102 × 72 cm

129 Hochschule für Gestaltung
und Kunst Basel (HGK Basel)
Jürgen Kaske
Winterhilfe
Secours Suisse d'hiver 95 –
Winterhilfe Schweiz 95 – Wintertime
assistance, Switzerland 95
1995 CH Offset 128 × 89,5 cm

130 Impuls Werbung AG
TBWA GGK
Caritas
Wegschauen. – Look away.
1999 CH Offset 170 × 117,5 cm

131 Ecole d'Art de La Chaux-de-
Fonds (EA)
Hervé Stadelmann (1978–)
Winterhilfe
www.soccorso-d-inverno.ch
2005 CH Siebdruck – Screenprint
128 × 91 cm

132 Sophie Rogg (1989–)
Winterhilfe
www.winterhilfe.ch
2007 CH Offset 170,5 × 117 cm

133 Hochschule für Gestaltung
und Kunst Luzern (HGK Luzern)
Julia Kaltenbach (1983–)
Winterhilfe
Armut geht unter die Haut
Poverty gets under your skin
2009 CH Offset 128 × 89,5 cm

134 Dimitri Reist (1986–)
Hochschule der Künste Bern (HKB)
Die Freiheit nehm ich Dir /
Im Gefangenenlager Guantanamo
werden zur Zeit 490
Männer teilweise seit Jahren
ohne Prozess festgehalten. (...)
I'm taking your freedom away /
Currently held without trial at the
prison at Guantanamo are 490
men, some for years ...
2006 CH Digitaldruck – Digital print
128 × 89,5 cm

135 Pierre Neumann (1951–)
Schweizerische Flüchtlingshilfe
(SFH)
Wohin würden Sie fliehen?
Where would you flee to?
1992 CH Siebdruck – Screenprint
128 × 90,5 cm

136 Marty Petersen
Visual Concepts International Inc.
Alles was ich will ist Weltfrieden
und...
All I want is world peace and...
1989 US Offset 61 × 91,5 cm

137 Masuteru Aoba (1939–)
Friede im Käfig – Peace in the cage
1982 JP Offset 76 × 103 cm

138 Masuteru Aoba (1939–)
Das wahre Gewicht von Frieden
The real weight of peace
1982 JP Offset 103 × 73 cm

139 Masuteru Aoba (1939–)
Die Energie ist für den *Frieden*
Energy is for *peace*
1982 JP Offset 103 × 73 cm

140 Shigeo Fukuda (1932–2009)
International Poster Biennial Warsaw
Sieg – Victory
1975 JP Offset 103 × 73 cm

141 Gérard Paris-Clavel (1943–)
Gérard Paris-Clavel
– Qui a peur d'une femme?
– Wer hat Angst vor einer Frau?
– Who is afraid of a woman?
1997 FR Siebdruck – Screenprint
120 × 81 cm

Ausgewählte Literatur / Selected Bibliography

Artis (Ed.), *Pour les droits de l'homme. Histoire(s) Image(s) Parole(s),* Paris 1989.

Barthes, Roland, *Sade-Fourier-Loyola,* Frankfurt am Main 1986 / Berkeley 1989.

Blisset, Luther & Sonja Brünzels, *Handbuch der Kommunikationsguerilla,* Berlin 1997.

Graffenried, Michael von, *Michael von Graffenried: eye on africa. Fotografien aus Kamerun,* Basel 2009.

Franck, Georg, *Ökonomie der Aufmerksamkeit. Ein Entwurf,* München / Wien 1998.

Kristeva, Julia, *Fremde sind wir uns selbst – Strangers to Ourselves,* Frankfurt am Main 1990 – New York et al. 1994.

Musée de la publicité (Ed.), *40 ans d'affiches unicef,* Paris 1989.

Musée des arts décoratifs (Ed.), *Für eine Zukunft mit Zukunft. Plakate zum Thema Ökologie,* Lausanne 1991.

Nghi Ha, Kien, *Ethnizität und Migration,* Münster 1999.

Parin, Paul, Fritz Morgenthaler, Goldy Parin-Matthèy, *Die Weissen denken zuviel,* Zürich 1963.

Rauch, Andrea & Gianni Sinni (Ed.), *SocialDesignZine,* Vol. 1, Florenz 2005.
–––, *SocialDesignZine,* Vol. 2, Florenz 2007.

Reschke, Kai & Reinhard Schultz (Ed.), *Frieden und Umwelt. Politische Plakatkunst aus den USA,* San Francisco 1986.

Salvemini, Lorella Pagnucco, *Toscani – Die Werbekampagnen für Benetton 1984–2000,* München 2002.

Sarfis, Thierry (Ed.), *L'eau pour l'humanité. Création d'une banque d'images*, Paris 1999.

Sontag, Susan, *Regarding the Pain of Others,* New York 2001. / *Das Leiden anderer betrachten,* München / Wien 2003.

Toscani, Oliviero, *Die Werbung ist ein lächelndes Aas,* Mannheim 1996.

Verband der Grafik-Designer e. V. & Verein für Kommunalwissenschaften e. V. Berlin (Ed.), *Wi(e)der Gewalt. Plakate gegen Gewalt und Fremdenhass,* Berlin 1993.

Ville de Chaumont, Alain Weil (Ed.), *Affiches politiques et sociales. Sixième rencontres internationales des arts graphiques,* Paris 1995.
–––, *L'engagement politique et social. Onzième rencontres internationales des arts graphiques,* Paris 2000.
–––, *Qui commande ? Douzième rencontres internationales des arts graphiques,* Paris 2001.

Dank / Acknowledgments

Publikations- und Ausstellungsprojekte sind immer ein willkommener Anlass, den eigenen, umfangreichen Bestand an Plakaten themenspezifisch zu sichten und aufzuarbeiten, aber auch durch gezielte Akquisitionen zu aktualisieren. Für die vorliegende Publikation haben wir zahlreiche Plakate von Gestalterinnen und Gestaltern erhalten. Ohne ihre grosszügigen Zusendungen wäre der zeitgenössische Fokus der Publikation nicht möglich gewesen. Ebenso danken wir ihnen für wertvolle Anregungen und Informationen zum Thema.

Publication and exhibition projects are always welcome occasions to examine and work with our own extensive holdings of posters with a specific theme in mind, and also to update it with targeted acquisitions. We have received large numbers of posters from designers for the present publication. Without their generous contributions, the contemporary focus of this publication would not have been possible. Our thanks go to them as well for their valuable suggestions and for providing information on the topic.

Sønke Gau
Geboren 1972. Kurator, Kulturwissenschaftler
und Autor (Zürich).
Born in 1972. Curator, cultural studies scholar, and
author (Zurich).

Katharina Schlieben
Geboren 1973, Kuratorin, Kulturwissenschaftlerin
und Autorin (Zürich).
Born in 1973. Curator, cultural studies scholar, and
author (Zurich).

Sønke Gau und Katharina Schlieben arbeiteten zusam-
men als kuratorisches Team der Shedhalle Zürich
(August 2004 bis Juli 2009, www.shedhalle.ch). Lehr-
aufträge an verschiedenen Schweizer Kunsthochschulen.
Regelmässige Veröffentlichungen in Kunstzeitschriften/
Publikationen. Aktuelle gemeinsame Publikationen
(Hg): *Spektakel, Lustprinzip oder das Karnevaleske?*,
bbooks 2008 und *Work to do! Selbstorganisation in
prekären Arbeitsbedingungen*, Verlag für moderne Kunst
Nürnberg 2009.
Sønke Gau and Katharina Schlieben worked together
as a curatorial team for the Shedhalle (August 2004
to July 2009) (www.shedhalle.ch). Teaching positions
at various Swiss art academies. Regular publications in
art journals and publications. Current publications
include *Spektakel, Lustprinzip oder das Karnevaleske?*
(bbooks 2008), and *Work to do! Selbstorganisation in
prekären Arbeitsbedingungen* (Verlag für moderne Kunst
Nürnberg 2009).

Bettina Richter
Geboren 1964. Studium der Kunstgeschichte, Germanistik
und Romanistik in Heidelberg, Paris und Zürich. 1996
Dissertation über die Antikriegsgrafiken von Théophile-Alexandre Steinlen. 1997–2006 wissenschaftliche
Mitarbeiterin in der Plakatsammlung des Museum
für Gestaltung Zürich. Seit 2006 Kuratorin der Plakatsammlung. Nebenbei Tätigkeit als Dozentin an der
Zürcher Hochschule der Künste sowie als freischaffende
Autorin.
Born 1964. Studied art history, German, and Romance
languages in Heidelberg, Paris, and Zurich. 1996 dissertation on the antiwar graphics of Théophile-Alexandre
Steinlen. From 1997 to 2006 served as a research
associate in the Poster Collection of the Museum für
Gestaltung Zürich, and as curator of the same since
2006. Also lectures at the Zürcher Hochschule der Künste
and works as a freelance writer.

Eine Publikation des Museum für Gestaltung Zürich
Christian Brändle, Direktor

A Publication of the Museum für Gestaltung Zürich
Christian Brändle, Director

Help!
Konzept und Redaktion / Concept and editing:
Alessia Contin, Christina Reble, Bettina Richter
Gestaltung / Design: Integral Lars Müller
Übersetzung / Translation: Ian Pepper (Ger.–Eng.)
Lektorat Deutsch / German Copyediting: Angela Kuhk
Lektorat Englisch / English Copyediting: Jonathan Fox
Lithografie / Repro: Lithotronic Media GmbH
Druck / Printing: Konkordia GmbH
Einband / Binding: Josef Spinner Großbuchbinderei GmbH

Reihe / «Poster Collection» Series
Herausgegeben von / Edited by
Museum für Gestaltung Zürich, Plakatsammlung
Bettina Richter, Kuratorin der Plakatsammlung /
Curator of the Poster Collection
In Zusammenarbeit mit / In cooperation with
Christina Reble, Publikationen / Publications
Museum für Gestaltung Zürich

© 2009
Zürcher Hochschule der Künste,
Zürcher Fachhochschule und Lars Müller Publishers

Museum für Gestaltung Zürich
Ausstellungsstrasse 60
CH-8005 Zürich / Switzerland
www.museum-gestaltung.ch

Museum für Gestaltung Zürich
Plakatsammlung / Poster Collection
CH-8005 Zürich / Switzerland
plakatsammlung@museum-gestaltung.ch

Lars Müller Publishers
CH-5400 Baden / Switzerland
books@lars-muller.ch
www.lars-muller-publishers.com

ISBN: 978-3-03778-174-6
Erste Auflage / First Edition 2009

Printed in Germany

Wir danken für Unterstützung
For their support we thank: